ASPECTS OF YORK

ASPECTS *of* YORK

DISCOVERING LOCAL HISTORY

Edited by
Alan Whitworth

Wharncliffe Books

First Published in 2000 by
Wharncliffe Books
an imprint of
Pen and Sword Books Limited,
47 Church Street, Barnsley,
South Yorkshire. S70 2AS

For up-to-date information on other titles produced under the
Wharncliffe imprint, please telephone or write to:

    Wharncliffe Books
    FREEPOST
    47 Church Street
    Barnsley
    South Yorkshire S70 2BR
    Telephone (24 hours): 01226 - 734555

ISBN: 1-871647-83-5

A CIP catalogue record of this book is available from the
British Library

Cover illustration: City Walls, York. *Courtesy of the Alan Whitworth collection*

Printed in Great Britain by
Redwood Books, Trowbridge, Wiltshire

CONTENTS

INTRODUCTION

by Alan Whitworth

WITH THIS PUBLICATION of *Aspects of York*, Wharncliffe Publishing continues in its tradition of issuing well crafted, well researched history books. From humble beginnings in 1993, with the publication of *Aspects of Barnsley*, edited by Brian Elliott, the *Aspects* series has grown into a library of many volumes covering almost the entire county of Yorkshire from the east coast to its western borders. The numerous books in the series represent over 200 articles by local authors on every aspect of local history; economic history, social history, popular culture, historical biography, environmental history, landscape history, medical history, transport and military history, the history of religions, oral history, architectural history... the list of topics is almost endless.

Diversity is the key word, and this first volume of *Aspects of York* is no exception, bringing together as it does a wide variety of studies in local history to the attention of the general reader. They are all written by local experts and keen amateurs with long experience of researching their subjects with an intimate knowledge of the sources that will illuminate and expand the secrets of their chosen topic, and illustrated with a bewitching array of maps, diagrams, photographs and other illustrations, many never before published. The articles should have a strong appeal to long-time residents of York and newcomers alike.

Social and scientific history is covered in articles by Alma Brunton, and Martin Lunn, who looks at the life and work of Thomas Cooke, York optometrist. Modern history is contained in the history of Elvington aerodrome during the Second World War and its later conversion to an air museum, and any book on the City of York would be incomplete without some reference to the great Minster Church of St Peter. In this volume, Ben Chapman describes the lost misericords there that have disappeared through fire and wanton destruction.

Landscape and architectural history are also well represented in this work. Alan Whitworth takes a perambulation around the walls and bars of York and in another article covers the story of the bronze plaques situated around the buildings and streets, telling of their history, and presenting them as a fascinating story book of the city's events and chronology. Sister Gregory Kirkus IBVM, provides a well researched glimpse of the founding and growth of the Bar Convent with which she is associated.

Lastly, no *Aspects* book is complete without some family history or biography. Eileen Rennison's childhood memories of York will no doubt bring back similar recollections to many readers. The story of the infamous Jonathan Martin is presented by Peter Howorth, while the life of an even earlier York resident, Margaret Clitherow, is told by the late Katherine Longley, one-time archivist at the Minster Library. For nature lovers, the day-book journal of the Welbourne family of father and son, provides a fascinating insight into their ornithological rambles around York and district discovering the bird life therein.

Finally, this volume could not have been produced without the help and assistance of a number of individuals and organisations. On the production side, Roni Wilkinson and Paul Wilkinson have made my job a lot easier and therefore deserve my sincere thanks. I would also like to express my gratitude to all at Wharncliffe Books involved in the promotion and support services for the book, including Managing Director, Charles Hewitt and in particular Imprint Manager, Mike Parsons and Paula Brennan for sales and promotion. I am also indebted to Brian Elliott, overall series editor for his invaluable suggestions. I should like to end this catalogue of thanks by expressing my appreciation to all the contributors who have written excellent articles that will hopefully inspire others to research *Aspects of York* for the benefit of future generations.

1. ASPECTS OF YORK

by Alma Brunton

BY THE SEVENTEENTH CENTURY, York was dominated by a tradition of its own antiquity and beauty. This tradition has, in part, been handed down to our own day in spite of the enormous losses of much of the physical content which had been the origin of this idea of the city. Both depression and prosperity have taken their toll of York: depression by allowing the churches and houses to decay beyond repair; prosperity by providing the finances for rebuilding and for that kind of development in which men speculate to accumulate. The great period of depression lasted from about the year 1400 until the reign of Queen Elizabeth I, when there was a partial recovery. The fact that in 1680, as reported by Keepe, it was one of the cheapest cities of Europe undoubtedly meant that there was then another wave of at least relative depression; and in the early nineteenth century there was a further economic recession from which York was saved by George Hudson and his manipulation of the railway network of the period.

It is a striking fact that adversity, rather than prosperity, leads to real as opposed to fallacious progress. The lonely stand of the United Netherlands in the sixteenth and seventeenth centuries, the regeneration of Denmark after the disastrous defeat of 1864, and latterly, the resurgence of Germany following the Second World War, are well-known examples of this function. The growth of the British Empire can be traced back to the final loss of Bordeaux in 1453 more than to any other single factor: out of despair arose a new hope and fresh ambition. The converse is now self-evident: never in the whole of recorded history has mankind appeared so bankrupt as in the recent age of growth and the so-called affluent society.

The application of these general principles to the special case of the city of York is of outstanding interest. Economic depression hung over it like an almost perpetual thundercloud after it had lost its last chance of becoming a major capital, possibly even the chief city of England in substitution for London, around the year 1398. The downfall of Richard II, the visionary sovereign who had dreamed of escape from the purse strings of the Lombard Street of his day, forever crushed the aspirations of the northern metropolis. Even the concept of York as the eponymous home of what, by magical coincidence, became the Yorkist and legitimate cause, was cruelly overthrown when the severed head of Richard, Duke of York, crowned in paper, was set over Micklegate Bar in midwinter of 1460. The following March saw the triumph of Richard's son, as King Edward IV, but the gay garden planted by the 'fair rose and herb' was not to be in York.

Necessity is the mother of invention, and it is to York's necessity that we owe a great deal in what may broadly be termed the field of applied science. This will become clear as we study the leading personalities of the city in the modern age - the three centuries that have passed since the Revolution of 1688. There is, of course, nothing sacrosanct about the Revolution in itself. It happens to mark a division more clearly than any other event within the great transformation of England that began at the Restoration of 1660 and the effective transfer of responsibility to Horace Walpole as Prime Minister between 1721 and 1730. Certainly it was within that overall period that York acquired most of the attributes that belong to the modern world. An effective piped water supply was installed between 1677 and 1685, official street lighting was introduced, a public bath-house opened in 1691, the General Post Office established, and a regular service of stagecoaches to London started in 1703. The environs were improved by planting trees in Lord Mayor's Walk in 1718 and on the Baile Hill in 1722 and 1726, and by forming the New Walk in 1731. The earliest newspaper, the *York Mercury,* began in 1719, to be followed in 1725 by the more famous and successful *York Courant.* The Mansion House and the Assembly Rooms were erected, and in 1727 an act was passed for improving the navigation of the Ouse. The Friars' Gardens, taken over in 1695 by George Telford, were becoming under his son John the most important nursery in the north of England and, as the historian Drake put it, bringing 'our northern gentry into the method of planting and raising all kinds of forest trees, for use and ornament'.

What particularly distinguished York from other cities at that period, however, was the practice of medicine. It was the home of a long series of physicians, surgeons and apothecaries of distinction. Between 1740 and 1743 it obtained the first general hospital north of the river Trent, a bequest of Lady Elizabeth Hastings (1682-1739), and so became the main teaching school, in medicine and anatomy, outside London. Whereas the capital had been fortunate in saving both its great medieval monastic hospitals for the sick, St Bartholomew's and St Thomas', at the Dissolution, York had altogether lost its magnificent double foundation of St Peter's and St

Leonard's hospital in December 1539. Nevertheless, York made up for this in the eighteenth century, not least because it already had the benefit of several outstanding medical men. Among the first of these was Dr Robert Wittie (1613-84), who practised here for twenty years before moving to London, publishing there in 1660 a book on *Scarborough Spaw*. Martin Lister, already mentioned as a scientist, became physician to Queen Anne. Clifford Wintringham (1689-1748), who built what is now the Judge's Lodgings, exercised his profession in York for thirty-five years and was the first physician to the County Hospital (Figure 1). Wintringham's successor as occupier of the house in Lendal, Dr John Dealtry, 'whose skill in his profession was only equalled by the humanity of his practice', died while visiting his patients in 1773 at the age of sixty-five.

The first honorary surgeon to the County Hospital was Francis Drake, the historian of York, City Surgeon from 1726. He was deprived in 1745 for refusing to take the Oath of Fealty to the Government at the time of the '45 Rebellion. Like his colleague Dr John Burton, the gynaeocologist and author of *Monasticon Eboracenes*, Drake was a strong Tory with Jacobite sympathies. The two antiquaries, at that crucial time, set out together to survey 'some Roman Curiosities, found in a Field near Millington, on the Wolds'. As Drake recorded, 'whilst we were upon the Spot & Directing this Survey, in the Year 1745, a Year in which the House of Stuart again attempted to recover the British Crown, some People observing us, gave Information at York, that we were marking out a Camp in the Wolds; which had like to have occasioned us some Trouble to contradict'. Burton was actually imprisoned in the Tower of London for a time and there met Flora Macdonald. Burton followed up his acquaintance and obtained from her first-hand details that he published in 1749 as *A genuine and true Journal of the most miraculous escape of the Young Chevalier*. In 1751 he brought out in two volumes *An Essay towards a complete new System of Midwifery*, a pioneer work with copperplates drawn and etched by the young George Stubbs.

Stubbs, born in Liverpool in 1724, was a self-taught painter and at the age of twenty had set up at Leeds as a portraitist. He must have realised that his knowledge of anatomy was inadequate and moved to York to take

Figure 1. The County Hospital, rebuilt between 1849-51 by J.B. and W. Atkinson.

advantage of the newly opened hospital. He learned anatomy from dissection, then uncommon, and from Charles Atkinson, another of the York surgeons, so well that Stubbs soon obtained employment as a lecturer to York medical students. He spent nine or ten years in York and it was there that he first conceived the idea of the studies in comparative anatomy, beginning with the horse, that proved in time that he was one of the great naturalists of the age as well as a supreme painter. His work for Burton, immature as it is, nevertheless demonstrates his deep and passionate search for the complete truth in representation. Dr John Burton and his book were savagely attacked by the ruling clique of Whigs, and purely from political odium. The Reverend Sterne's cruel caricature of 'Dr Slop' reflects as much discredit upon its author as credit to the victim, whose ungainly body hid a noble heart. In an age of little charity Burton rode long rounds to visit the sick poor and justified himself by saying: 'I will at any time very willingly do my best to save any person, especially the poor and helpless: to do this I think is my duty and everyone's whom God hath enabled to do it.'

John Gowland, born in the parish of St Martin, Coney Street, in 1704, was apothecary to King George I and George II and spent most of his life away from York but two other apothecaries, father and son, spent most of their lives there. They were Theophilus Garencieres (1715-84) and Theophilus Davye Garencieres (1742-1803), who practised in Blake Street and was Lord Mayor in 1796. They were descended from the great French doctor, Theophilus Garencieres (1610-80), who took his degree at Caen but on becoming a Protestant settled in England. Two more surgeons should be mentioned: James Atkinson (1759-1839), the son of Charles, a founder of the Yorkshire Philosophical Society and of the York Musical Society as well as a book collector of note and Sir William Stephenson Clark, Lord Mayor of York in 1839, who had a resplendent residence in Micklegate. We should also not forget Dr Stephen Beckwith the philanthropist who lived on Bishophill; his grandiose tomb in the Gothic style is in the Minster.

Finally, before leaving the subject of medicine, something should be said of The Retreat, the Quaker institution for the care of the mentally afflicted (Figure 2). Founded by William Tuke (1732-1822), a prominent grocer in the city (Figure 3), he was one of the fourth generation from the first Tuke Friend who had joined George Fox in the middle of the seventeenth century. The unsatisfactory treatment of the insane moved Tuke in 1790 to consider the possibility of establishing something better for their care, run by

Figure 2. The original Retreat, instituted in 1795. *From a painting by Cave.*

Friends for Friends. Land was purchased in 1793 on a splendid hilltop site towards Heslington, plans were obtained the following year from John Bevan, and the building was opened in 1796. The great superiority of the methods used at The Retreat was recognised from the start and in our own times L.A.G Strong has written that 'a powerful, tranquillising spirit pervades these walks and walls and gardens'. Among the superintendents of The Retreat was Dr John Thurnam (1810-73) who was not only a leading authority on insanity but an outstanding anthropologist. The Retreat was by no means the only York institution set up and endowed by the Tuke family. In 1784 they originated the girls' school now The Mount, and in 1818 a boys' school which became Bootham School in 1829 (Figure 4). Medicine is an applied science which makes the most obvious impact on the average human life, but it was only one aspect of the flourishing technological life of York during this period. Some of the skilled crafts of the Middle Ages represented the beginnings of later York industries. The entire history of one of these crafts, that of horners and combmakers, has been traced and written about by the late Mr L.P. Wenham, from the year 1295 when it was already in being, down to 1931 when it came to an end with the firm of Rougier, established about 1794 and the source of the name of Rougier Street, well known in connection with the York bus station. The detailed story of the York clockmakers and watchmakers with a list of them from 1471 until the mid-nineteenth century has been

researched by T.P. Cooper. The Poll Tax of 1381, not in print in Cooper's time, carries the tale back for almost another century, to John Lovell, 'orlogemaker', who was living in the parish of St Mary, Castlegate with his wife Agnes. Lovell had taken up the freedom of the city in 1374, but as a

Figure 3. A drawing of William Tuke, Quaker, founder of Bootham School.

Figure 4. Lady Johnstone's Mansion, in Bootham, c.1838, to which Bootham School moved in 1846.

goldsmith. The association between the crafts of goldsmith and silversmith and that of clockmaker has of course continued, in York as elsewhere. In York there was an assay office for silver from 1561 and important pieces of plate were made until soon after 1700, but the York mark has not been found between the years 1713 and 1778, and from that date onwards York silverware was of comparatively little importance. The city's most famous clockmaker was Henry Hindley; the last of the famous silversmiths and watchmakers were the partners James Barber, Lord Mayor in 1833, and Robert Cattle, Lord Mayor in 1841, whose business premises were in Coney Street.

Another York trade that has been studied in depth is that of the bell-founders. They formed one of the most notable of the technological crafts and were already flourishing at the start of the fourteenth century. The greatest of the family firms was that of Oldfield, which flourished from 1588 to 1650, when it was succeeded by the Smiths already established in a foundry at Toft Green, who continued until 1731; and the Seller family. Their foundry was at Jubbergate, in the centre of the city, and lasted from 1662 to 1764. The last York bell-founder was George Dalton, with premises in Stonegate and later in Lendal. He flourished from 1750 until 1791. Interestingly, no sooner had bronze-founding died out than iron-foundries were set up in York, a city not previously noted for this industry. The most important of these iron-foundries was that of the Walker family, who had the Victoria foundry in Walmgate.

The making of various types of musical instruments appears to have been an offshoot of the several metal-working trades. At the end of the eighteenth century there were a number of plane-makers, among them

Michael Varvill, who was at first in High Ousegate but later removed across the bridge. In connection with plane-making, it should be remembered that, apart from the simple joiner's plane, complex moulding planes were made which enabled panelling, picture-frames and other details to be produced economically. Plane-making, as a consequence, played a vital role in connection with building and cabinet-making and preceded the modern machine-tool industry of the late nineteenth century. The important York glass industry, producing bottles, jars and many other commercial products including scientific glassware, was founded in 1794 by John Prince (1749-1835), a jeweller, who was the son and grandson of York bricklayers and builders. A later development of this industry was the production of optical lenses and telescopes, microscopes and other instruments, by Thomas Cooke. He started his business in 1837 and by 1856 was able to build the large Buckingham works on the site of the Duke of Buckingham's house on Bishophill. As Thomas Cooke & Sons Ltd the firm continued and eventually formed part of the amalgamation Cooke, Troughton & Simms, which became internationally renowned.

Quite another side of applied science is represented in York by the wholesale trade in pharmaceutical drugs. This presumably grew out of the strong medical interests of the city and was perhaps also connected with the concentration of gardens and nurseries in York from an early date. One unique relic which survives from the medieval compounding of drugs is the magnificent bronze mortar of the infirmary of St Mary's Abbey, cast by Brother William de Touthorp in 1308 (Figure 5). First mentioned in 1734, by Thomas Gent, the mortar was lost for many years but was eventually secured for the Yorkshire Museum. The drug trade of more recent times begins with George Ewbank, already a druggist in Castlegate by 1738, the year of birth of his son George. The son carried on the business after his father retired to take up banking and the firm, after passing through several partnerships, joined that founded in 1818 by John Raines which, in 1897, had taken over Micklegate House. A third York business in the same field was begun in Colliergate in 1780 by John Dales, Lord Mayor in 1816 and 1829; this later became Butterfield & Clarke and then Bleasdale Ltd. A glimpse of the background of the trade in earlier times is given in the obituary of Duke Holborne, a York gardener who died at the age of seventy-seven in 1837. Holborne had been a Blue Coat boy, was then apprenticed for seven years to Robert Young, a well-known city gardener, and took up the freedom in 1787. He held positions as a gardener with various families, but 'for many years eked out a living by selling herbs to druggists'. In more modern times, the pharmaceutical trade has continued with the establishment of the research laboratories of Smith and Nephew at Heslington.

Figure 5. An engraving of the infirmary mortar, 1308, from St Mary's Abbey.

The gardens of York were of great importance to the economy and reputation of the city from an early date even after London became the main centre of the nursery business in England. It is impossible to distinguish between the various types of gardening before the year 1700 or thereabouts and many of the recorded gardeners probably kept market gardens for the supply of vegetables to the city. Starting in 1334, gardeners took up the freedom, and three were mentioned in 1381, as well as fruiterers who in all probability grew the fruit they sold. As has been mentioned, the Friars' Gardens on the site of the Dominican precinct - and very likely the garden of the ancient royal palace before 1227 - were leased by George Telford from 1695 and had a continuous history until the railway took over the ground for the Old Station. This nursery was only the chief of several that flourished in the eighteenth century, significantly in the former precincts of other religious houses. The family of Bearpark had part of the site of St Mary's Abbey (Figure 6); a succession of gardeners had the Trinity Gardens off Micklegate and Thomas Rigg took part of the land that had belonged to St Andrew's priory in Fishergate. The Whartons, who had held the lease of the Friars' Gardens before the Telford family, moved to the Grey Friars below Castlegate. It was reported in the *York Courant* of 20 March 1760 that on the previous night Matthew Wharton's garden had been broken into by some person who 'cut down 463 Elms, from five to twelve feet high; 335 Cherry stocks; 4 Damsins; 19 standard Pears; and cut up part of a large Flat of Pease.' Rewards offered by Wharton and later, in the *London Gazette,* by the town clerk, do not seem to have produced any information as to who the culprits were.

The interest in the purely ornamental side of gardening goes back a long way. There was a Florists' Feast held in 1740 at Gibson's in Lendal, and in 1742 at Gainford's in Goodramgate, when a gold ring was the prize for the best carnation. The first of these was probably Henry Gibson, a somewhat shadowy figure who took on several

Figure 6. St Mary's Abbey, now in the grounds of the Yorkshire Museum.

apprentices between 1733 and 1754; the other was Francis Gainford or Gainforth who took up the freedom in 1713 and in 1729 supplied trees for the Lord Mayor's garden and Common Hall Yard, behind the newly built Mansion House. He was a churchwarden of Holy Trinity in 1752 and still living in 1758. It is not known whether there was any formal organisation of these early florists, but on 20 April 1768 there was founded what is now known as the Ancient Society of York Florists, a body that brought together amateurs and professionals and men from all classes of society. The first signature on the roll was that of surgeon Charles Atkinson and other early members included John Telford junior, John Roebuck, William Adcock, Thomas Halfpenny, Joseph Perfect, and Andrew Thompson, nurserymen, and head gardeners; the botanist Robert Teesdale from Castle Howard; T.D. Garencieres the apothecary; the younger George Ewbank from Castlegate and James Wiggins of Pavement, another druggist. Detailed rules were drawn up and frequent shows were held for hyacinths, auriculas, polyanthus, tulips, ranunculus, and carnations in their seasons.

The interest in gardening, combined with the long tradition of printing in York, produced a small crop of books on the subject. The first, by John Kennedy who was gardener to Sir Thomas Gascoigne Bart, was *A Treatise upon Planting, Gardening, and the Management of* the *Hot-House*, published in 1776; then William Speechley, gardener to the Duke of Portland, brought out two standard first class works, *A Treatise on the Culture of the Pine-Apple* in 1779, which he followed with *A Treatise on the Culture of the Vine*, in 1790. Next came the book of an amateur dilettante, Richard Steele, *An Essay upon Gardening,* issued in 1793. Dr John Evelyn's *Sylva*, was reprinted in 1776 at York, with additional notes by Dr Alexander Hunter who practised in the city from 1763 and was the real founder of the York lunatic asylum in Bootham Park, begun in 1772 and opened five years later. Though the books were illustrated with engraved plates, they were not of outstanding botanical interest. It was not until a much later work, David Wooster's *Alpine Plants*, published in 1874, with over one hundred coloured plates drawn from specimens obtained from the York nursery of Backhouse & Son, that a major step in the correct delineation of plants took place.

There was a surprising gap in the succession of York artists during much of the eighteenth century. Francis Place died in 1728 and was the last survivor of his age (Figure 7). In that same year John Haynes became free as a saddler, but took up engraving and land surveying. In 1740 he advertised that he printed on leather for saddlers and surveyed land, and also 'draws Perspective Views of Gentlemen's Seats'. Haynes carried out archaeological surveys as well as estate plans and, after moving to London about the year 1750, he published the valuable engraved plan of the Chelsea Physic Garden and in 1755 made a large survey of Burghley Park for the Earl of Exeter. The noted portrait painter Philip Mercier, born in Berlin of Huguenot parents but settled in London, moved to York and was resident there from 1739 until 1759 in the Minster Liberty. Apart

Figure 7. A drawing of York Minster, c.1705, by Francis Place.

from occasional visits by artists of national fame, such as that of Turner in 1797, York was singularly lacking in painters and draughtsmen for over a century.

This state of affairs changed with Thomas Beckwith, the herald painter, who employed his friend Edward Abbot to make drawings of York buildings, but his work was crude. However, quite suddenly a group of York draughtsmen caught up with the same goal, appeared within a short time: Joseph Halfpenny, Henry Cave, and John Browne. Halfpenny was a remarkable pioneer in the portrayal of medieval architecture, but it was rather Cave who was typical of the York tradition in that he came from a family steeped in the technique of whitesmith's work and was the son of an engraver, William Cave (1751-1812), who had been the apprentice of Robert Holme or Holmes, Ledger's brother-in-law and successor in Petergate. Henry Cave's etchings of *Picturesque Buildings in York*, issued in 1813, is the best single record of the old city. Like Browne, the historian and artist of the Minster, Cave earned his living largely as a drawing master.

The city's great tradition of glass-painting, from far back in the Middle Ages, continued through the seventeenth century in the persons of Edmund and Henry Gyles, to its final revival by the idiosyncratic career of William Peckitt. During the eighteenth century York was also the home of a family of distinguished sculptors, the Fishers. Their pedigree is mysterious, since few of them left wills, and they moved from one address to another. Furthermore, they were prolific and repeatedly employed the same Christian names. What is certain is that the first carver of the family, Richard Fisher, moved to York from Ripon in 1746 after executing works at Leeds, Ripon, and for country houses including Studley Royal where the chief gardener and clerk of works, William Fisher (died 1743) was probably his father. Richard had married Alice Broadley at Ripon in 1730 and by her had several children, of whom John Fisher the elder (1735-1804) was likewise a noted statuary. At least ten of the family, over four generations, worked as sculptors in York, and in the last generation they also produced an architect, Charles Fisher (1829-92) who was the articled pupil of George T. Andrews, friend of George Hudson, and who was responsible for much railway architecture in the county. Fisher designed the new chancel of Holy Trinity, Micklegate, in 1886.

The architects of York in the eighteenth century and the early nineteenth century are numerous and distinguished. The most interesting practice, which still survives today, is the one handed down from John Carr 'of York' through a long succession of partnerships: with Peter Atkinson the elder, his son of the same name, the latter's sons J.B. and W. Atkinson, and so on down. Carr's greatest contemporary in the city was Thomas Atkinson (1729-98), no relation to Peter, who was the son and grandson of bricklayers and who is particularly remembered for his work at Bishopthorpe Palace undertaken between 1763 and 1769. He also erected for himself a fine house in St Andrewsgate, no.20. His best work by far in York, however, is the Bar Convent of 1765 to 1775 with its main frontage built between 1786 ann 1789. Among the later architects, alongside G.T. Andrews, was J.P. Pritchett. Both were involved in the architecture of the early railway age, and both were among the last outstanding exponents of Georgian classicism, along with J.B. and W. Atkinson.

John Carr, though not born in York, was a Yorkshireman and of such surpassing fame that his career deserves more than a passing mention. His origin is well-known, thanks largely to the detailed researches of Robert Davies finished shortly before his death in 1875. Carr was born at Horbury near Wakefield in 1723, the son of Robert Carr a stonemason and quarry-owner, and was himself trained as a working mason. In early life he married Sarah Hinchcliffe of Felkirk in Scotland, more than ten years older than himself and said to have been in domestic service at Bretton Hall where Carr was employed at the time as one of the masons. In his youth John Carr was certainly poor, for he used to say: 'I have many a time had to lie in bed whilst my breeches were mending.' Within a few years, however, he was getting commissions. The first of these to bring him near to York came in 1749-50 when he built a new front and added a stable block to Askham Richard Hall, one of the country seats of the Garforth family, whose town house was at no.54 Micklegate. Carr was already living in the city of York by 4 October 1751 when he bought his first piece of property, a house 'with a Raff Yard, Garth, and a Kiln' in Skeldergate for £180. He described himself at that time as 'mason', and was put down as 'stone-cutter' when he took up the freedom in 1756. This was just after he had erected the grandstand on the Knavesmire to his own designs, chosen in 1754 in preference to those of James Paine. When, in 1765, he purchased a much larger Skeldergate property for the sum of £580 he was calling himself an architect. Apart from his professional career Carr played a prominent role in civic affairs, as chamberlain in 1766, sheriff the next year, alderman in 1769, and twice Lord Mayor in 1770 and 1785. Many anecdotes are told of Carr's cheerful and powerful personality, and of his fine singing voice. In 1789 at York races, attended by the Prince of Wales and the Duke of York,

Carr was asked to entertain the royal visitors and 'delighted the company by singing with admirable spirit and sweetness, the well-known patriotic ballad called 'Hearts of Oak'.

The architectural and building craftsmen of York between the years 1700 and 1850 were numerous, but the most important of them formed veritable dynasties. Among the carpenters and joiners, some of whom also took up bricklaying and contracting, there were five generations of the Etty family, four of the Hansom family culminating in Joseph Aloysius, who was responsible for the Hansom cab, six generations of the Raisin or Rayson family, from Richard Rayson free in 1664 to his great-great-great-grandson Thomas Rayson (1792-1828). In another line of descent the original Richard's grandson Richard Raisin (1712-1801) was said at his death to have been '60 years a master builder in York'. The bricklayers could show three generations of Clough, as many of Fentiman, and four generations of the Gray family; and the stonemasons included three generations of Kilvington and two of the Stead family. Many of these men undoubtedly designed, with the assistance of copy-books, the houses they put up, and it is to them that a very high proportion of the sound construction and seemliness of the streets of York is due.

It is perhaps unnecessary to say much of the great tradition of York printers and booksellers (Figure 8), for Robert Davies devoted a whole book, *A Memoir of the York Press* (1868), to the authors, printers, and stationers from 1497 to 1789, and T.P. Cooper studied both 'The Sign of the Bible' in Stonegate and 'The Sign of the Crown' in Minster Gates, two of the greatest of York bookshops. York's first printer was Frederick Freez, 'a Dutchman and alien enfranchised', made free of the city in 1497 and in 1506 ordered to dwell upon the common ground at the *Rose*, otherwise the *Bull* in Coney Street for ten years; but by 1515 he was living in the parish of St Helen on the Walls in Aldwark. Frederick's son Valentine, free as a cordwainer in 1538, was a Protestant martyr, burned alive on the Knavesmire at the same stake with his wife, a deed attributed by Fuller to Edward Lee, 'the cruel archbishop'. Among later printers in the city the most famous, deservedly, is the eccentric Dubliner Thomas Gent (1693-1778), who settled permanently here in 1724 and took over a noted press in Coffee Yard. Gent left an autobiography,

Figure 8. William Alexander's printing and publishing house, Castlegate, one of the many famous printing houses of York.

published in 1832, but in his own time was particularly known for his work *Ancient and Modern History of the famous City of York*, which he brought out in 1730, anticipating Drake by six years. Gent was not a scholar, but in this and his later histories of Ripon and Hull he displayed great powers of detailed observation which have given his books permanent value as a record of much that would otherwise be unknown.

The York trade in books was of immense value, and reached its peak at the 'Bible' in Stonegate under John Todd from 1762 until 1811. Todd, who at first had Henry Sootheran (later Sotheran) as his printer, in 1766 launched a circulating library of several thousand books on all subjects. Subscribers of three shillings a quarter or twelve shillings a year could have two books at a time and change them as often as they pleased, but they could only have one new book at a time for up to six days; other books might be kept for a month. Non-subscribers were allowed to borrow books by paying 6d for a copy of the catalogue and at the rate of one shilling for a folio, 6d for a quarto, 3d for an octavo and 2d for a duodecimo, for one week, with an extra charge of 3d for a fortnight and 4d for three weeks. This commercial lending library was replaced in 1794 by the Book Society, which grew into the Subscription Library and lasted until 1918. York was slow to adopt the measures of the *Public Libraries Act,* resolutions being defeated by polls of the ratepayers in 1881 and again in 1887 before winning through in 1891. The first public library, in Clifford Street, was opened by the Duke of York (later King George V) on 4 October 1893.

John Todd had been apprenticed to John Hildyard, an earlier owner of 'the Bible', and stayed on as assistant to Hildyard's successor John Hinxman who at the end of 1759 published the first two volumes of Laurence Sterne's *Tristam Shandy.* No bookseller in London was prepared to take the risk of issuing the book, which was then considered ridiculous and unsaleable. Sterne hawked the copy around his acquaintances in York and eventually, as John Croft the wine merchant and antiquary wrote, 'a Mr Lee a Gent[n] of York and a Batchelor of a liberall turn of mind lent him one hundred pounds towards the printing [of] the Work'. Hinxman sold two hundred copies in two days and the great London publisher Dodsley then agreed to bring the book out, as was announced in the *London Chronicle* of 1 January 1760. The identity of Sterne's benefactor, Mr Lee, was for a long time a mystery, but he has been identified as William Philip Lee, the wealthy descendant of an ancient Buckinghamshire family, who had settled in York by 1760 and died

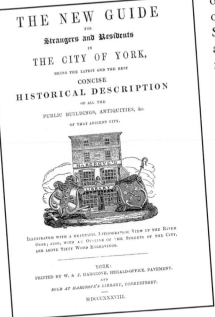

Figure 9. The title page to the *New Guide... to the City of York,* published by W and J Hargrove, who ran one of the many nineteenth century subscription libraries, shown on the title page.

on 12 March 1778 at the age of seventy-one. Lee subscribed to the first volume of Sterne's sermons, also published in 1760, and eventually settled in what was then a modern house, no.40 Blossom Street, demolished in 1965 despite being under the protection of a Building Preservation Order. After his death, Lee's library was said to comprise many valuable items 'in every class of Literature, and in most Languages' (Figure 9).

York of the eighteenth century not only appreciated books: it also had a successful theatre. There had been a theatre in York for generations, and there had been a commission as early as 1629 for William Perrey to keep a company of players to be known as His Majesty's Servants for the City of York. Previously to that, there had been a tradition of theatricals in the city from the Middle Ages, and York was already famed for its cycle of Mystery Plays performed in the streets, albeit these stemmed from religious roots. At the opening of the eighteenth century plays were staged in the upper room of the Thursday Market House (Figure 10) in what is now St Sampson's Square, and then in the tottering old hall of the Archbishop's Palace behind the Minster. The first permanent theatre erected for the purpose was put up in 1744 on the site of the present Theatre Royal, which has thus had a continuous history for over 250 years. This theatre was occupied by Joseph Baker's Players so successfully that Baker was able in 1764 to begin building a larger theatre around the old building, without closing. By good fortune Baker was soon afterwards able to obtain the services of Tate Wilkinson (1739-1803) as a member of his company, and made him manager in 1768. Wilkinson took over the theatre on the death of Joseph Baker in 1770, having already obtained for it in the previous year a patent as the Theatre Royal, York. Ever since then the York theatre has been a proving ground for actors and actresses, and has welcomed famous ones, from Mrs Siddons in 1776 onwards. Tate Wilkinson wrote an autobiography and played himself down with the phrase: 'If I had held my pen but half as well as I have held my bottle, what a charming hand I should have wrote by this time.' But his fame was based on his humanity and honesty as much as on his gifts: when he died it was said that 'owing to his kindness to his performers, his judicious instructions, and his punctuality in pecuniary matters, his dependents considered him more as a father than a master. He excelled both as a tragedian and a mimic, and as a theatrical tutor he was never equalled.'

The chapter closes full on music, but of the music of York and in York there is no space to write adequately, and so I shall just end by mentioning briefly that the Minster has, of course, an immemorial tradition of organs and choir. The first organist of note

Figure 10. An engraving of the Thursday Market, in which, on the upper floor plays were performed.

was John Thorne, a writer of motets and reckoned by Morley as one of his authorities. Thorne died in 1573 and was buried in the nave of St Peter's. The great organ was built between 1632 and 1634 by Robert Dallam, citizen and blacksmith of London, just in time to be heard by Lieutenant Hammond on his visit. Of his experience he wrote 'we saw and heard a faire high Organ, newly built, richly gilt, caru'd [carved] and painted, a deep and sweet snowy Crew of Quiristers [choristers].' Ten years later the organ was leading the singing against the noise of the Parliamentarian bombardment, so poignantly recollected by Mace in *Musick's Monument*. 'The Enemy had planted their Great Guns so mischievously against the Church... that sometimes a canon bullet has come in at the windows and bounc'd about from pillar to pillar...'; but 'they had then a custom in that church (which I hear not of in any other cathedral) which was always before the sermon the whole congregation sang a psalm together with the quire and the organ... This organ... being let out into all its fulness of stops, together with the quire began the psalm. But when that vast-concording unity of the whole congregational chorus came (as I might say) thundering in... it made the very ground shake under us... .'

In conclusion, the term modernity is a relative word and shifts perpetually with the march of time. Historical objectivity cannot be achieved in less than three generations or say one hundred years and this may excuse us from attempting to follow the story of York and its social and architectural structure beyond mid-Victorian times. In spite of the social and cultural activities of the Georgian period and the great and public-spirited aspirations of many of its citizens, York for a generation after 1800 was a city of much misery and want. After the wartime boom had ended at Waterloo in 1815 the whole country plunged into mass unemployment and a chasm of depression, sliding, with occasional recoveries, towards the Hungry Forties. This was a national graph of deep-seated disease in the body politick, but the attack was particularly severe in York.

In the remaining streets of the period we can observe a serene front, of brick or stucco, typically it may be by the design of Peter Atkinson the second and the building craftsmanship of Thomas Rayson the first: South Parade or St Leonard's Place. Town planning, first exemplified back in the eighteenth century by the street improvements at St Helen's churchyard and Blake Street, at Spurriergate and Nessgate, at the foot of Goodramgate and in King's Square, beside St Crux, was beginning to take hold of the city. These changes were marked on the plan published in 1785 by Ann Ward in her abbreviated and revised edition of Drake's *Eboracum;* 'the several places dotted thus shew where the Streets have been widened by the public spirit of the Corporation'. Such alterations spread and became the order of the day: the walls, bars, and posterns were threatened, the posterns and three barbicans taken down; in 1806 the castle moat was filled and Castlegate Lane widened; between 1810 and 1820 Ouse Bridge was rebuilt; the new House of Correction erected on Toft Green. In 1821 Low Ousegate and Spurriergate were widened, in 1827 St Peter's Gate to the Minster Yard was pulled down, and in 1831 the walls breached and St Leonard's Place begun. Two years later the grandiose clearance started for the new market place of Parliament Street. All this cost money, yet York did not really have any superfluity of wealth. Nonetheless, great cultural schemes were put in hand: the Yorkshire Philosophical Society was launched in 1822, and in the following year the first of the great musical festivals in the Minster (three more were to follow in 1825, 1828 and 1835). In 1825 the City Improvement Commissioners were appointed, in 1827 the York Footpath Association was formed to save and repair the walls. The area of the Museum Gardens, part of the King's Manor, was granted to the Yorkshire Philosophical Society as a botanical garden and as a site for a museum, and in 1830 the Yorkshire Museum was opened. A year later, the national organisation the British Association for the Advancement of Science was formed, at the suggestion of Sir David Brewster, but with the Yorkshire Philosophical Society as its exemplar, and with Canon William Venables Vernon Harcourt of York as its mentor and first Secretary, the Association acknowledged its parentage by holding its first meeting in 1831 in York.

Politically, the whole country was in a state of upheaval, and the *Reform Act* passed in 1832, was followed in 1835 by the *Municipal Corporation Reform Act,* which tore away the old Ainsty and gave it to the West Riding, and abolished the old corporation with its closed shop. This was, in principle, intended genuinely to open the way to free enterprise. Whereas, for instance, the York Gas Company had laid its mains in 1832, dissatisfaction at its prices enabled a rival body to be floated, the York Union Gas-Light Company of 1837. Competition between the two companies lasted for six years before amalgamation, and brought the gas rate down from ten shillings to 6s 8d per 1,000 cubic feet by 1849; but the consumers then unavailingly pointed out that the average in other towns was only 4s 6d. York was certainly not altogether a cheap city. At the same time its population was rising at a tremendous rate, from under 17,000 in 1801 to 19,000 ten years later, reaching nearly 22,000 in 1821, and over 26,000 by 1831. In 1841 there were almost 29,000 inhabitants. During the Napoleonic Wars few houses were built, and, as a result, overcrowding took a hold, climbing from an old average of a little under six persons per house to 7.17 in 1811. Thereafter, however, it declined to a level average of five from 1841 onwards, when the inhabited houses in the city numbered 5,768.

Unlike the greater towns of the West Riding and of the north generally, York had not been much affected by the growth of factories and the Industrial Revolution, but some side effects began to manifest themselves. In 1816 the first steamboat was put into service between York and Hull and greater changes were portended, regionally, by the start made on Goole docks in 1820. By 1832, two years after the successful opening of the Liverpool and Manchester Railway, schemes for railways to York began to be discussed. Three years later, in the year of the passing of the old corporation, the new age was signalled by the establishment of the York and North Midland Railway Company. In 1839 the first train ran, and by the summer of 1840 there were four trains to London every day and the journey had been reduced to ten hours. By 1842 the last stagecoach had run. The railway reached Newcastle in 1844 and Scarborough in 1845. In 1854 a vast amalgamation took place of the lines directly concerned with York traffic, resulting in the formation of the North

Eastern Railway, which covered most of Yorkshire, the whole county of Durham, and a great deal else.

This fantastic revolution in transport was due to the march of invention and in Britain was universal in scope. There was no real argument about the fact that the era of the horse was past and that steam was speedily taking its place in all aspects of life, from transport to motive power in agriculture, industry and the home. But in rail transport there was a whole world of doubt as to where the principal lines would run and where the vital junctions would be placed, the ganglia of the trade and industry of the future. In some cases there already existed towns and cities of such overwhelming industrial importance that they were quite inevitably the centres of development and, in this, Manchester and Birmingham are two names that spring to mind. In other instances small towns of no importance became great railway centres, Swindon or Crewe for example. The case of York was quite different. The city was, economically, in a very poor way and in comparison with Leeds or Hull virtually powerless. It had its historic past and its prestige as the notional second city of the realm and imaginary capital of the north, but in the age of industrial civilisation these counted for nothing.

The course of the history of York was changed at the crucial moment by one man alone, George Hudson (Figure 11). The brain and hand were his, and the weapon of £30,000 of capital was put into his hand by his fortunate legacy of 1827. Despite what has been written and said about him over the centuries, there is no doubt that Hudson, ambitious as he was, was a fundamentally honest man with a disinterested desire to improve the position of York and of his fellow citizens. Sincere patriotism has seldom been found in such concentrated form or carried to such extreme lengths. As soon as the possibility of railways appeared on the horizon, Hudson realised the potential of this new form of transportation, and made it his business to learn all about it, to meet George Stephenson the engineer and the early promoters in the north of England. It was upon Stephenson that Hudson urged that he should 'mak all t'railways cum to York', and when Stephenson would have none of it - seeing no value in traffic to the effete city - Hudson determined to go it alone. By almost

Figure 11. George Hudson (1800-71) as a young man.

superhuman efforts on committees of the old and new corporations over a period of years, then on boards of company after company and working at prospectuses and draft bills for Parliament, he achieved his end. York, with no obvious advantages except its geographical position in a level plain, did become the greatest railway centre of its region and the central node on the main route from London to Edinburgh (Figure 12). In a time of frenzied promotion of more railways than the country could hold or pay for, Hudson promoted almost exclusively lines that made sense. True, in the course of the general mania he manipulated accounts and cut corners to keep his railroads from bankruptcy. And when the crash came it was Hudson, as the most prominent figure of the era, who received most of the blame and virtually all of the disgrace; yet he was not fraudulent and was never prosecuted; indeed, he was so beloved in the north-east that he was re-elected as MP for Sunderland for another ten years. Many others, some of them a great deal higher up the then strict social ladder, were equally blameworthy, but Hudson never named them. Charles Dickens asked a friend why he stuck to Hudson: 'Because he had so many people in his power, and held his peace.' Ironically, the railways that George Hudson promoted did not fail as countless others did, and virtually all went on from strength to strength and survived to the present day; possibly the most fitting epitaph for this most misunderstood man of the period.

Hudson was an altogether exceptional person, but though the part he played was essential, he was only one of a number of men who, in the York trade of the nineteenth century, made their mark. His original trade was a linen-draper, a member of one of the less characteristic businesses of the city (Figure 13). More typical middlemen dealt in butter and bacon, tea and cocoa, confectionery

Figure 12. The interior of York Railway Station, designed by Prosser, Burley and Peachey, and opened in 1877. It was the largest railway station in the world at that date.

Figure 13. The front of St William's College, showing the Regency shops. It was in one of these in the foreground that George Hudson had his drapery business.

and toys. The butter trade was due to the existence in York of the legal staple: all butter from the Ouse valley as far south as the river Wharfe, if packed in firkins for export wholesale, had to be brought to the Butter Market in Micklegate 'to be viewed searched weighed and sealed' and appropriate dues paid (Figure 14). The old butter stand, where this was undertaken, stood on the frontage of the churchyard of St Martin-cum-Gregory and was rebuilt about 1778, only to be demolished fifty years later when the trade ceased. In Drake's time the export of butter from York was 60,000 firkins a year, rising to 80,000 by 1780 but dropping to less than 15,000 firkins by 1818. The firkin of butter was reckoned at half a hundredweight. The placing of the Butter Market on Micklegate Hill resulted in that district having a concentration of merchants who dealt in dairy products, bacon and provisions.

Dealing in tea, coffee, cocoa and sundries was quite a different business, and most of it was done on the other side of the river. Interestingly, not only the beverages alone were sold over the counter of these trades, but commonly also the cups in which they were consumed: hence the curious description found in early directories and in Dr White's plans, of 'Tea and China-man'. A good deal of this trade was in the control of Quakers, notably the Tuke family. It is not generally realised that the great York firm known as Rowntrees came into being through the division of the much older business of the Tukes, founded in the second quarter of the eighteenth century. Their tea trade moved to London, and the cocoa and chocolate side was taken over by the brothers Henry Isaac and Joseph Rowntree, sons of Joseph Rowntree the first (1801-59). The old Tuke shop was in Castlegate, not far from the Coppergate premises which housed the later confectionery business of the Craven family, famed for their mints. The third great York firm famous for sweets started in 1767 and for two generations belonged to the family of Baildon or

Bayldon. Later partnerships with Robert Berry of St Helen's Square and with Joseph Terry led to the noted firm of Terrys, which continued under four later generations of the same family.

With perhaps some spiritual kinship to the confectionery trade is the trade in children's toys. By 1798 the title 'toyman' was applied in the *Universal Directory* to John Barber of Coney Street, John Bell in Stonegate who also sold snuff, John Jameson of College Street, John Lund of Goodramgate, and George Stones of Spurriergate. By 1823 the number of toy manufacturers and warehouses had risen to nine, as well as William Morritt of Feasegate, a toy turner. Of the nine, three were mainly wood turners, one a turner of brass, iron and ivory as well as wood, another a jeweller, one a trunk maker, one a comb maker, and one a basket maker; while Martha Marshall of 16 Coney Street was a manufacturer of fishing tackle, jewellery, cabinets and spinning wheels.

From the cradle to the grave, York was also a great centre of monumental masons. Besides the firms of sculptors, such as the Fisher family, there were humbler yards that produced many hundreds of gravestones and tablets. They and their products, with the epitaphs inscribed, have been studied by J.B. Morrell in his books *York Monuments* and *The Biography of the Common Man of the City of York as recorded in his Epitaph*, the latter probably the first representative collection made for a single city and spanning the years from the Roman period to recent times. Throughout the nineteenth century the yards which did most business were those of Plows at Foss Bridge and Skelton in Micklegate. There were three generations of the Plow family, beginning with Benjamin (1765-1824) who worked for twelve years as a mason at the Minster, and his son William Abbey Plows (1789-1865). The extremely prolific Matthew Skelton appears to have been a father (1772-1844) and son

Figure 14. An engraving of the Butter Stand as it stood in Micklegate before demolition in 1828.

(1798-1878) of the same name, trading firstly from what is now no.25 Micklegate on the south side of the street, and later behind no.64 in the yard running back to Tanner Row.

Some of the masons, to judge from the doggerel of their epitaphs, may have composed the verses they inscribed on the memorials; others may have been scribbled down by a mourning relative, or simply taken from a volume of poems and plagarised, like the odd version of Dryden's *Hymn for St Cecilia's Day* on a stone in the churchyard of Holy Trinity, Micklegate, to Adam Bowlby who passed away in 1819. Inside the church on the south wall is a medieval inscription to 'Walterus Flos' alias Walter Flower, a member of the family of St Robert of Knaresborough (died 1235), son of Took Flower, twice Mayor of York in the earliest days of the mayoralty under Richard Coeur-de-Lion. St Robert, dying elsewhere, has left no monument in York, and this applies to others of her most famous sons: Miles Coverdale, probably born here in 1488, and John Flaxman, certainly in 1755. In a rather different category of fame is the son of the Skeldergate ferryman Edward Bowling, proved by George Benson and the late Miss Isabel Pressly to have been the Lieutenant in the Royal Navy whose death in 1797 was immortalised by Charles Dibden's poem:

> *Yet shall poor Tom find pleasant weather*
> *When He who all commands*
> *Shall give to call life's crew together*
> *The word to pipe all hands;*
> *Thus death who Kings and tars despatches*
> *In vain Tom's life hath doff'd;*
> *For tho' his body's under hatches,*
> *His soul is gone aloft.*

Born in York; married in York, like Vanbrugh; died in York: three categories of men, overlapping yet distinct. Many of those born in the city, whether of old families or of mere passing strangers, like Flaxman, go away to live and die elsewhere. Others, not of York born, come from afar, like Martin Soza the Spanish goldsmith, born in Sapher (Zafra), free of the city in 1529, chamberlain in 1534 and sheriff in 1545, who was buried in the Minster in 1560. The personal motives of the moves are seldom known, and what we see are glimpses of the unexpected. In our course through the city and its past we have seen again and again that this is the one true constant: in York one may expect nothing but the unexpected. Whatever the future may hold for York, it will come as a surprise.

2. THE LOST MISERICORDS OF YORK MINSTER

by Ben Chapman

YORK MINSTER (Figure 1) once possessed a fine Gothic choir with a set of sixty magnificent misericords. Alas all but two of these misericords were destroyed by an act of arson in 1829 by one Jonathan Martin.

Martin was born in 1782 near Hexham in Northumberland. He was the brother of Jonathan Martin the celebrated painter of large allegorical canvasses, and William Martin, a noted philosopher. Around the year 1810 he joined the Wesleyan Methodist Connexion, where he developed a strong antipathy toward the Church of England. He disapproved of the clergy who often attended balls and parties, and displayed his resentment by frequently interrupting church services.

On 1 February 1829, Jonathan Martin secreted himself in York Minster where that same night he deliberately set fire to the choir stalls before making his escape. It was not until the early hours of the following morning that the fire was noticed and the alarm called. However, it continued to rage until it was finally put out in the afternoon. The roof of the central aisle, tabernacle work, the choir stalls, galleries, pulpit and the Bishop's throne, were all completely destroyed (Figure 2).

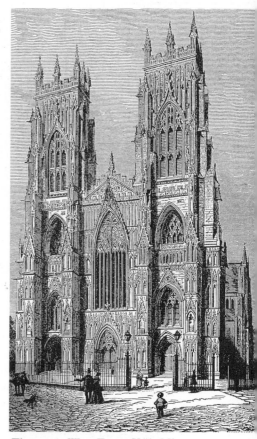

Figure 1. West Front, York Minster in the nineteenth century.

Martin (Figure 3) was subsequently arrested, tried, and incarcerated on the grounds of insanity. He was committed to St Luke's Hospital, in London, where he died on 3 June 1838.

Figure 2. South transept of York Minster following the modern-day fire of 9 July 1984. *Alan Whitworth.*

Of the sixty misericords dating from the late fifteenth century, only two survived the inferno and have remained until the present day, and can now be seen in the Zouche Chapel in the Minster.

The definition of a misericord is a small projecting bracket on the underside of a stall seat in a church. Such stall seats were fitted with a hinge so that when turned up, the bracket - or misericord - formed a shelf that could be used as a rest or seat to ease the suffering of tired, aged and infirm priests during the extremely long hours they were obliged to stand in their devotions. The protruding bracket thus enabled the cleric to rest his bottom and so support his bodily weight on the edge of the upturned seat, giving the impression that he was still standing. Hence the name misericord

Figure 3. A contemporary engraving of Jonathan Martin as he appeared during his trial.

Figure 5. A misericord showing an elephant in St Mary's church, Old Malton. *Alan Whitworth.*

Figure 4. Choir stalls in the former priory church of St Mary, Old Malton. *Alan Whitworth.*

Figure 6. One of two surviving fifteenth century York misericords. *Ben Chapman.*

from the Latin word for 'an act of mercy'.

Originally misericords were to be found where there was a collegiate foundation (Figure 4). At the Dissolution of the Monasteries in the sixteenth century during the reign of King Henry VIII, many were destroyed, whilst others were recycled and put to use in some smaller parish churches.

Often these misericords were carved and decorated, and because they were for the most part hidden, woodcarvers were traditionally allowed a great deal of freedom in the subject matter. Many, in fact, contain visual puns and humorous scenes, others are quite licentious and show rude pictures, while a great number depicted everyday scenes of medieval social life (Figure 5).

Of the surviving misericords which can be seen in the cathedral church of St Peter, commonly called York Minster, one depicts a splendid eagle with elevated wings facing the right support, and

Figure 7. A set of four evangelical symbols from a medieval brass rubbing.

holding in its beak a long blank scroll, the other end of which is held beneath the left claw (Figure 6). The two side supporters are carved as roses. It is known that one of the badges attributed to the Duke of York was an eagle. The eagle and scroll were also the symbols of the evangelist St John. The evangelical emblems of the four saints which apart from the winged eagle of St John are a winged lion (Mark), ox (Luke) and angel (Matthew), are quite commonly depicted on misericords, and usually appear in sets (Figure 7).

The second misericord (Figure 8) shows a squatting figure supporting the bracket on his shoulder and upraised hands. The man is wearing a tight long-sleeved jerkin with buttoned front, and over this a long loose tunic with elbow length loose sleeves. He also wears

Figure 8. The second surviving misericord in York Minster. *Ben Chapman.*

Figure 9. Misericord in Lincoln Cathedral showing a wife fighting with her spouse. *Ben Chapman.*

a cape, and a Phrygian-style cap and pointed shoes of the period. The two supporters are grotesque lion masks.

Sadly, none of the other sixty misericords survives, but there still exist engravings in the eighteenth century book *Gothic Ornaments in the Cathedral Church of York* by Joseph Halfpenny, published in 1751, which shows two further misericords.

One depicts a woman in a long loose tunic with her head covered. She grasps a man similarly clad by the beard, as she prepares to strike him with a washing implement known as a 'beetle'. The two supporters are grotesque lion masks, like those on one of the surviving York misericords. Such scenes of domestic discord are quite common, and in Lincoln Cathedral there is a similar example dating from the late fourteenth century (Figure 9).

The other engraving shows a seated cleric or schoolmaster 'birching' a miscreant on his bare back. The left support depicts a seated dragon-like creature, while the right shows a large dog-like demon being held fast in the jaws of a grotesque lion mask.

Any reader wishing to see fine sets of misericords in Yorkshire are recommended to visit Beverley Minster (1520), Ripon Cathedral (1489), St Mary's Church, Beverley (1445) and one of the oldest in England in the church of the Blessed Virgin Mary, at Hemingborough, which dates from the thirteenth century.

3. Springtime Saunters

Introduced and edited by Alan Whitworth

IN THE EARLY 1950s, during my youth, I avidly collected the eggs of wild birds. My collection was extensive and scientific, insomuch as each egg was confined to its own separate compartment in a cabinet drawer, cocooned in cotton wool, and meticulously labelled in a childish hand on a strip of paper. Among a select few neighbourhood 'amateur naturalists' we roamed the countryside for miles to find new nest sites, we swapped eggs, and we bragged about the number and variety we held - scoring points against our fellow 'collectors' for the rarities.

Yet even then as a hobby, it was becoming increasingly frowned upon among a certain level of society labouring to bring an awareness and increasing respect for wildlife to the rest of us. I recall a period of afternoon 'detention' doled out by an enlightened school headmaster for being in possession of a robin's egg purloined from a nest in a hedgerow within the school grounds. Then there was the time I received some 'parental guidance' on the subject in the form of a good smacking when, having climbed a large mature hawthorn tree, I inadvertently broke a tawny owl's egg in my best Sunday suit pocket as I came down from on high - 'although I can't help but feel that playing truant from Sunday School had more to do with the punishment than my parents respect for the preservation of fowls of the air!

Today, all birds in the wild are protected in Great Britain at all times with few exceptions. The general scheme for their protection is to create offences for killing, injuring, or taking birds, and for the taking, damaging or destroying of nests or eggs, and having possession of birds, nests or eggs. There are also offences concerned with selling them under the *Wildlife and Countryside Act, 1981* - and any person found guilty of any such acts against a bird or its eggs is liable to a summary conviction with a penalty of a fine not exceeding one thousand pounds and forfeiture of any bird, nest or egg.

How times have changed! One hundred years ago the picture was entirely different - 'bird-nesting' was big business - and a small catalogue I recently unearthed in a local York bookshop entitled, *British and Foreign Birds' - Skins and Eggs*, issued by H.W. Marsden lists literally hundreds of different species and their eggs for sale (Figure 1).

Dated 1893, the foreward states, 'With the issue of this catalogue, I beg to thank all my many friends and customers for the cordial support given to me during the past twenty-one years... it is revised to the end of 1892, and all prices have been carefully considered and fixed as low as possible to supply thoroughly good and reliable specimens... . Since my removal from Gloucester to Bath, three and a half years ago, my business has greatly increased, and Mr Joseph Mountjoy (late of Gloucester) has recently entered my sole and permanent employment. He takes on the entire management of the taxidermy department, and I respectfully ask that any work of this kind you may wish done may be entrusted to me, as I can confidentially guarantee first class and artistic treatment thereof... .'

Glancing through the pages, it is interesting to note the prices of several common birds' eggs offered for sale by Mr Marsden's establishment at that date; thrush, 1d; hedge sparrow, 1d; robin, 1d; winchat, 3d; garden warbler, 2d; chiff-chaff, 3d; jackdaw, 2d; jay, 4d; turtle dove, 4d; wild duck, 2d; teal, 6d.

Such was the popularity of this hobby that even as little as twenty years before my days, the story was similar, and it was not unusual to find adults happily engaged in 'bird-nesting'. Another recent find was that of a small day-book or journal inscribed with the name Eric H. Welbourne, and a number of addresses. Covering the period from 1915 to 1946, it details the excursions that Eric and his father, Walter Robert Welbourne made around York and the Yorkshire Wolds in search of nests, and carefully lists the numbers of eggs and birds they discovered on their travels.

The first address, 36 Stonegate, York, is where Walter Robert Welbourne traded in antiques and lived with his wife Minnie and family. However, by the year 1946 his son, Eric Welbourne, was

Price 1d ; Post Free 1½d.

A PRICED CATALOGUE

OF

BRITISH AND FOREIGN

BIRDS'-SKINS & EGGS

ANIMAL SKINS,

European & other Lepidoptera

BRITISH & FOREIGN SHELLS,
CABINETS, TAXIDERMISTS' TOOLS,
BOTANISTS' REQUISITES, STORE BOXES
AND APPARATUS OF ALL KINDS
FOR THE USE OF STUDENTS OF NATURAL HISTORY

ALSO SOME OF THE MOST USEFUL

BOOKS ON NATURAL HISTORY SUBJECTS.

N.B.,—Ova, Living Larvæ, or Pupæ of Insects are not dealt in.

H. W. MARSDEN

(Late of Gloucester),

21, NEW BOND STREET, BATH.

Bath, January, 1893

Figure 1. The cover of Marsden's catalogue of Birds'-skins and eggs.

resident in the village of Little Horton, on the outskirts of Bradford in the West Riding, living at 25 Elizabeth Street after moving from Markham Crescent, Haxby Road, where he was in 1932. Later in 1946 Eric moved to Ripon, and took up residence at 5 Westbourne Grove, the last address. Yet together, for all the distance between the two, father and son still made regular trips to their old haunts around York; although from 1930 onwards they appear to be less daily and more monthly. Finally, only occurring annually, probably undertaken during their yearly holiday from employment, and the pages of this small pocket-book meticulously detail each outing.

1915 April 6. Between Hayton and Nunburnholme Station. Thrush 3. Thrush 2.

1915 April 18. Round Heworth nearly to Holtby and back by Stockton Lane... Water Hen (ready for laying). . . 18 eggs.

1915 April 21. Up Malton Road about five miles and back... Plover (ready for laying)... 11 eggs.

1915 April 24. Round Stockton Lane nearly to Holtby and back by Heworth. . . Greenfinch, same as had none on 18th. Saw every nest that I found on 18th... 12 eggs.

1915 April 25. About $3^1/_2$ miles up Malton Road and back...9 eggs.

1915 May 7. Round Stockton Lane nearly to Holtby and back by Heworth. Chaffinch 2, same as had none on 18th... Heard the Cuckoo singing for the first time. 7 eggs.

1915 May 8. To Stamford Bridge by train, then to Buttercrambe by river and back same way. . . Blackbird, 5 young ones. Water Hen, 7 eggs and 1 young one. Blackbird 5 young ones and 1 egg. Blue Tit, 7 [eggs]. Snipe 4 [eggs]. Jackdaw [eggs]... 2 Ring Doves [eggs]. . . 47 eggs 16 young.

1915 May 9. Down Elvington Lane and back. Chaffinch 1 [egg]. Greenfinch 4 [eggs]. Linnet 5 [eggs]. 10 eggs.

1915 May 22. To Wheldrake by train and back to Elvington, then came back to York with train... Whitethroat 5 [eggs]. Pheasant 8 [eggs]. Pheasant 5 [eggs]. Thrush 4 young. Thrush 4 young.

1915 May 24. [Whit Monday]. Train to Stamford Bridge, by road to Buttercrambe, Bossall, Howsham Bridge, back by water past Scayingham to Stamford Bridge. Hedge Sparrow 4 + 1 Cuckoo [egg]... Willow Wren 7 [eggs]. Jenny Wren 6 [eggs]... Barn Owl (eggs). Spotted Flycatcher 2 [eggs]... 136 eggs 40 young.

1915 May 30. Dunnington Lane off Stamford Bridge road... Willow Wren 6 [eggs]. Blackbird (young). Yellow Hammer 2 [eggs]. Chiff-chaff 7 [eggs]. Yellow Hammer 3 [eggs]... 30 eggs 4 young.

Figure 2. Skylark *(Alauda arvensis)*.

1915 June 5. To Heworth, Tang Hall Lane, Osbaldwick Lane to Osbaldwick, Murton down Murton Lane to Sandy Lane, down Bramble Bush Lane across footstiles to Holtby Lane and on to Stockton Lane, down Hopgrove Lane onto Malton Road and back to York. 13 miles. Winchat 7 young. Whitethroat 5 [eggs]. Yellow Hammer 4 [eggs]...Winchat 4 [eggs]. Willow Wren 5 eggs + 2 young. Skylark 4 [eggs]... (Figure 2) Robin 4 young... Willow Wren 7 [eggs]. .. Partridge 12 [eggs]. Robin 4 young + 1 egg... Reed Bunting 4 young. 102 eggs. 30 young.

1915 July 21. At Hayton. Corncrake 2 [eggs] + Corncrake 1 [egg].

1916 April 16. Went to Hayton on bike with father and found... a Jenny Wren's nest, ready for laying.

1916 April 21. (Good Friday). Down Elvington Lane and off down Dunnington Lane. Thrush 4 (Black set).

1916 April 22. To Stamford Bridge by train, to Buttercrambe by water and back same way. . . Jackdaw (eggs) same as we saw last year. . . 36 eggs.

1916 April 26. (Wednesday). At Skelton Springs. Blackbird 2 eggs.

1916 April 29. To Stamford Bridge, our usual round. Snipe 4 [eggs]. Snipe 4 [eggs]. Hedge Sparrow 3 [eggs]. 11 eggs.

1916 May 10. Down Dunnington Lane by myself.

1917 April 22. Elvington Lane. Blackbird 2 eggs.

1917 May 6. Warthill Lane and Stamford Bridge.

1917 May 13. Holtby Lane and Stamford Bridge. . . Wild Duck 10 (Stamford Bridge in tree, side of Trout stream) (Figure 3).

1917 May 27. Up Malton Road to Little Grebe Pond, and lanes near

Figure 3. Mallard in flight *(Anas platyrhynchos)*.

by, down to Sand Hutton and Stamford Bridge, Buttercrambe Woods and Craggs, back by Warthill. . . Garden Warbler 4 [eggs]. . . Willow Wren 6 [eggs]. . . Jackdaw, young. . . Pheasant 2 [eggs]. Partridge 6 [eggs]. Wild Duck 9 young.

1917 May 28. (Whit Monday). Elvington Lane to the old barn in Dunningham Lane and back. House Sparrow 4 [eggs]. Ditto 5 [eggs] - both in the old barn under the eaves.

1917 June 3. Tang Hall Lane, Murton Lane to Murton, round lanes to Holtby Lane back over fields to Murton, back home by Osbaldwick. Tree Sparrow 3 eggs (in an old tree in Tanghill Lane). . . Partridge 16 [eggs]. . . Winchat 3 young + 2 eggs.

1918 May 25. To Skipwith Common by Escrick. Whitethroat. . . Yellow Hammer 4 [eggs]. Chaffinch 4 young. . . Robin 6 eggs.

1918 May 31. Old Barn and Dunnington Lane. Whitethroat 5 [eggs]. Tree Pipit 6 [eggs]. Swallow 4 [eggs]. Yellow Hammer 5 young.

1918 June 7. Old Barn and Dunnington Lane. House Sparrow 4 eggs + 1 young. Hedge Sparrow 4 eggs + 1 Cuckoo.

In the year 1919 it would appear that the two undertook no excursions. Possibly First World War intervened and prevented their rambles. A single entry for 1920 records 'Father and me April 18th. Robin with young.' Interestingly, the entries from 1930 are kept in a different hand, suggestive perhaps, that the small pocket book was first written by the father Walter Welbourne, then the duty was passed on to the son, Eric, particularly as the style of entry alters slightly.

However, as certain earlier entries infer grammatically that the son made these, possibly the notes were rewritten at a later date, as a loose page from another similar sized pocket book duplicates the entry for 5 June 1915.

1930 April 18. (Good Friday). Father by himself down Sandy Lane, back by Holtby Lane and Stockton Lane.

1930 April 20. (Easter Sunday). Father and I Tang Hall, Sandy Lane, Holtby Lane and Stockton Lane.

1930 April 26. Saturday evening. Water Lane and Rawcliffe Lane... Heard the Cuckoo for the first time and saw the first swallow...

1931 May 25. (Whit Monday). Bus to Dunnington Lane. Walked on main road toward Kexby one mile and turned down lane on right towards Wheldrake. Then walked two or three miles and turned right again down Elvington Lane where we caught bus home... Thrush sat. Chaffinch young. Blackbird sat... Hedge Sparrow 3 + 1 Cuckoo... Nest of fully fledged Linnets.

1932 May 15. (Whit Monday). Father and I by 'bus to Kexby Bridge, then on river side to Sutton Bridge, turned sharp right over bridge, skirted Elvington village and turned right again up lane past Mr Ryder's (of Leeds) estate on to Hull Road where we caught bus back. In second field at Kexby Bridge we saw Swan sitting but male bird drove us away... 42 eggs.

1932 June 5. Father and I by bus to Brickyard Lane, about half mile this side of Kexby, down lane and round into Elvington Lane. Yellow Hammer in hedge with young. Unusual position due to heavy rains, caused flooding in hedge bottoms. Greenfinch 2 [eggs]. Pied Wagtail with 3 eggs at back of haystack in field half-way down lane. Took snap. Blackbird 3 [eggs]. Willow Wren 4 [eggs] - took snap. Willow Wren 3 [eggs]. Linnet 3 [eggs] - took snap. Yellow Hammer 3 [eggs], took snap...

1932 June 12. Father and I to six mile post on Hull Road, down Brickyard Lane to Elvington and Sutton-on-Derwent and back same way. Saw nest we saw last week on same route and found that one of the eggs in the Wagtail's nest was Cuckoo's. The grass was saturated with rain that had fallen in the night and this prevented our searching the hedge-bottoms properly (Figure 4) but there was plenty of evidence of nests and we saw a Robin sat in a hole in a tree stump but there were no eggs in

Figure 4. A hedgehog searching the hedge bottoms. These nocturnal animals enjoy a meal of birds' eggs.

Figure 5. Raven *(Corvus corax).*

the nest. The Willow-Wren had laid one more egg each. . .

1933 April 30. The Stray, Wigginton Road, York. Hedge Sparrow 3 [eggs].

1933 May 21. Sunday. Father and I to *Barmby Moor Inn,* down Sutton-on-Derwent Lane on to Allerthorpe Common then on lane to Sutton Bridge and Elvington, down Kexby Lane on to Hull Road and back by bus; walking about eight miles. Whitethroat - ready for laying... Hedge Sparrow 5 young - nest in hole in Willow-tree like Willow-Wren's but could not see eggs. It's nest on side of haystack...

1933 May 28. By bus to Wheldrake, then walked to West Cottingworth and Thornganby and across Skipwith Common on to Escrick Road to Escrick. Swallows - ready for laying (in cowshed). Willow-Wren, young. Mistle Thrush - young (in fork of tree on Skipwith Common: parent birds made strenuous efforts to frighten us off). Blue Tit? Young - in hole in decayed Silver Birch [tree], apparently excavated by Woodpecker...

1934 May 16. To Skipwith by 'bus, across Skipwith Common, back by road through Skipwith village and round Crook Moor. Rain spoilt the day. Thrush sat. Wild Duck (not yet fully identified - may be Teal)

Figure 6. Rook *(Corvus frugilegus).*

10 eggs, black set - among dead bracken near pool of fresh water in middle of Common not far from road. (The above has been identified for us by the gamekeeper as a Teal)... Visited the gullery - swarms of Black-headed Gulls and Herring Gulls? Nest were in an inaccessible swamp - want waders.

1934 May 18. Skipwith Common... Teal, 9 eggs - not far from one found on Wednesday - among bracken but only found through diligent searching, as eggs were invisible, being covered, completely with down - bird not flushed...

1934 May 20. Skipwith Common... Pheasant 15 eggs in dried bracken in middle of Common. Shoveller - nest contained shells only, indicating that the clutch had been safely hatched... Pheasant 15 eggs - not far off the main road on the outskirts of Skipworth Common on Thorganby Road, in dried bracken like previous one.

1934 June 3. Skipwith Common (Back Common & Crook Moor). Jay 5 eggs (nest up Birch sapling about ten feet from ground, made of twigs...

1934 June 17. Skipwith Common (Back Common & Crook Moor)... Two Wood Pigeons, sat, but too high. Three Turtle-doves, sat, but too high...

1938 May 8. Skipwith Common... Pheasant - sat on eggs - did not disturb her. Saw two adder [snakes].

From hereon, there is not another entry until the year 1945, when only three appear, one of which reads, 1945 May 18. Friday night. Ripon - field adjoining Bishopton Bridge up Studley Road (with Mr George). Greenfinch 5 [eggs]. Blackbird 4 [eggs]. Greenfinch 5 [eggs]. Thrush 2 [eggs]. Blackbird 3 [eggs].

The lack of entries for the years 1939 to 1945 again no doubt reflects a disruption into their excursions by war years. At this time a Mr George makes his appearance as companion to Eric; undoubtedly Walter Welbourne, his father, was getting on in years, and possibly was ill or too infirm to get out and about into the countryside. It was soon after this that a penultimate and poignant entry in the journal reads, 'Father died June 24th 1946 - thus bringing our bird-nesting partnership to an end.' The next, and final entry reads - '1946 June 5. Ripon - Studley Road with Jean and Mr George. In nettles in quarry, Whitethroat 5 [eggs]. On roadside, Yellow Hammer, 3 [eggs]' - perhaps from this we can speculate that Mr George was the father of Jean, to whom Mr Eric Welbourne was possibly paying court!

4. MAD, BAD AND DANGEROUS - JONATHAN MARTIN THE YORK ARSONIST

by Peter Howorth

THERE HAD BEEN RUMOURS in York for most of the day that he had been caught near Ripon and was being brought back to York on the Carlisle coach. A crowd had gathered at the staging post, the *Black Swan,* in Coney Street. By the time the stagecoach had arrived at half-past ten that night there was a clamorous mob demanding to know which he was, pointing out suspects and shouting 'hang him!'It was an unpleasant and alarming experience for the unsuspecting passengers arriving, none of whom could have expected such a welcome.

In fact it was nearly three o'clock in the morning when a post-chaise delivered the prisoner to Peter's Prison near York Minster, described in 1838 as an 'old building, and disgraceful'and which at that time was noted for 'brutality and cruelty'. Despite the hour, a panel of magistrates decided to send for the witnesses and the press and to examine him straight away. In the Hall of Pleas above Peter's Prison which was reached via a flight of steps from the Minster Yard, he was cautioned that he need not say anything unless he pleased but that any observation he might make would be taken down and may afterwards be produced against him. Throughout his examination the prisoner remained calm, mild-mannered and cooperative. He volunteered a statement and spoke without displaying any emotion. Following this preliminary hearing, he was committed to the city gaol and taken there by coach at half-past six o'clock that morning. Even at that early hour, some thirty people had gathered to catch a glimpse of him.

Jonathan Martin was born in the year 1782 at Haydon Bridge, near Hexham, in Northumbrland. The son of William Fenwick and Isabella Martin, he was one of five surviving children of thirteen that his parents had. The other surviving children were William, born 1772 at Haltwhistle, philosopher and author of *The Philosophical Conqueror of All Nations,* Richard, born at Brig of Doon, Ann, born at Kilcolemceal at the south end of Kintyre and John, born 1789 at Haydon Bridge, a painter of note.

Jonathan was first apprenticed to a tanner at Darlington, but moved to London where he was press-ganged into His Majesty's Navy aboard the seventy-four gun ship HMS *Hercules* in 1804. Despite this unfavourable beginning he obviously made an effort, and by the year 1807 Martin was one of the captains of the fore-top aboard HMS *Atlas* at Copenhagen when the British seized the Danish fleet to prevent it falling under French control. It was there that he fell from the fore-top into the sea (Figure 1). He was immersed in the Baltic for twenty minutes before a boat lowered from the vessel could pick him up. Not surprisingly Martin was badly shaken by the incident and John Douglas, who served with him, felt that afterwards there was a change in his personality. Martin, nevertheless, continued to serve in the Royal Navy, taking part in

Figure 1. Jonathan Martin's Providential Escape from a Watery Grave in the Bay of Biscay. An engraving by Wm Martin in *The Life of Jonathan Martin, Tanner by Himself* (2nd Edition, 1826).

the evacuation of Corunna and seeing action at Lisbon. He deserted at Cadiz, sailing to Egypt in a merchant vessel, before being paid off six years later.

Returning to his home area as a farm labourer, Martin married, and a son, Richard, was born about 1813, but on the death of his mother, the boy was sent to boarding school. He was at school in Lincoln in 1829. Martin, however, appears to have remained in his native land, working for a Darlington tanner from 1822 until April 1825. He had the reputation of being a good workman but with a religious turn of mind. Notwithstanding his skill, around that time he was sacked from his profession and set out to earn his living by selling pamphlets of his life at one shilling each, first published in 1825. This was entitled:

The Life of
JONATHAN MARTIN,
OF DARLINGTON, TANNER
Written by Himself

containing
An Account of the Extraordinary Interpositions of Divine
Providence on his behalf, during a Period of Six Years Service
in the Navy, including his Wonderful Escapes in the Action
of Copenhagen, and in many Affairs on the Coast of Spain and
Portugal, Egypt, etc. Also, an Account of the Embarkation of
the British Troops after the Battle of Corunna. Likewise an
Account of his subsequent Conversion and Christian Experience,
with the many Persecutions he suffered for Conscience'Sake.

DARLINGTON:
Printed at the Office of Thomas Thompson,
Of the High-Row,
1825.

On the reverse of the title-page there appeared the following
advertisement:

*The author requests his readers to overlook the many grammatical
inaccuracies they are sure to meet with in the following sheets: and he
is in hopes he will secure their indulgence when he informs them that
he is only (as some of them know) an illiterate man, whose only means
of learning was by his own unaided efforts, while enduring the
confinement he is here relating. His aim in publishing this simple
narrative of his life, conversion and sufferings is the glory of God, and
should it be the means of encouraging one soul to set out for the
Kingdom, he will feel amply rewarded.*

Reasonably successful, he printed a third edition of 5,000 copies in
Lincoln, describing it as 'considerably improved, with engravings by
the author'(it also included drawings by his brother William). This
was a skill that ran in the family, for his brother John (1789-1854)
was a well-known painter and engraver, who was much admired for
a number of religious works in particular *Belshazzar's Feast* (1821)
which was considered his finest piece and won him £200 from the
British Institution and *The Fall of Nineveh*, exhibited in Brussels in
1833, where he was elected a member of the Belgian Academy and
given the Order of Leopold. His painting was marked by a wild
imaginative power, perhaps indicative of a family trait.

In October 1828, Jonathan Martin married Sarah Hudson aged
twenty-seven from Boston in Lincolnshire. He was described as
being kind and affectionate to his wife. For some reason they moved
to Yorkshire, lodging in York, Leeds and Hull. On 28 January 1829,

having conveyed his stock of books by stage wagon from York to Leeds, the couple took up residence at 6 Brick Street, Leeds. The following Saturday he left his wife in Leeds, telling her that he was going to sell his pamphlets in Tadcaster and that he would return on Monday. In truth, he returned to his old lodging at 60 Aldwark, York, the home of a shoemaker with whom he had previously stayed.

The Saturday afternoon Martin spent walking about in the Minster Yard and attended the Sunday service next day. He then hid in the Minster behind Archbishop Grenfield's monument until it was shut up by the sexton at half-past-six that night. He came equipped with matches, a razor and a pair of pincers that he had taken from the shoemaker's house. Climbing the stairs to the belfry, Martin cut a length of rope about seventy feet long from the prayer bell with the razor and knotted it into a rough climbing ladder. Next he cut off some crimson velvet, some gold fringe and two gold tassels from the Archbishop's throne and made them into a bundle that he took away. Using the wooden hoist used for cleaning purposes inside the Minster, known as the 'speed', he gained access to a window in the north transept, breaking it with the shoemaker's pincers, which he carefully left on the window-sill to be found. Fastening the rope to the iron stanchion of the window, he dropped it through on the outside as a means of escape. He then returned to the floor of the Minster to the boys' robing room of the choir, placed cushions and prayer books into piles, and set fire to them. When he was satisfied that the fire had taken hold, he used the hoist again to climb to the window and left by the rope which he had previously prepared.

The fire was discovered early on Monday morning 2 February, by one of the choristers, a boy named Swinbank, but by that time it was well established in the choir and was spreading towards the east window along the roof. The Minster's own fire engine proved ineffective but the one based at the army barracks in the city and the 'Yorkshire' fire engine were much more powerful. Pipes were taken to the roof of the choir, but despite this, the progress of the fire could not be checked. By nine o'clock that morning half of the choir roof had been destroyed and hundreds of workmen were trying to cut away the remainder of the roof in a desperate attempt to preserve the east window. Melted lead streamed down from the roof and the spouting on the walls. The limestone pillars of the choir cracked and split under the intensity of the heat, splintering to nearly half their original size. The silver of the communion plate melted into an unrecognisable mass. In such extremely dangerous conditions, the workmen were driven back and the central roof could not be saved.

A length of approximately 230 feet crashed in flames into the body of the church. By twelve noon the tabernacle work, the organ, the pulpit, the cathedra, and the choir stalls were entirely destroyed, and the roof had fallen inwards.

As soon as the extent of the fire was realised, messages had been sent to Leeds and Tadcaster for additional fire engines to be sent. The various insurance firms responded by sending their appliances, so that by four in the afternoon there were ten fire engines fighting the blaze. These included one from Escrick Park, pulled by four grey carriage horses of the local Member for Parliament for greater speed. The tower acted as something of a fire-break, helping to save the nave, but the area from the organ and the choir to the east bore the brunt of the conflagration and was totally destroyed. The great east window itself was not too seriously damaged, but it was late on Monday night before the fire was considered to be extinguished. Preliminary estimates put the cost of repairs at between £80,000 and £150,000.

Once the immediate threat from the fire was ended, people began to concentrate on the cause. The rope still dangling from the transept window left little doubt that the incendiary was started deliberately and attention quickly focused on Martin. It was recalled that a number of writings had been found about York Minster in the previous few months. A stone, left in the west aisle on the 16 January, was wrapped in a copy of *The Life of Jonathan Martin*. Another letter, dismissed at the time as of no importance, the work of a crank, took on a new significance.

'A Just Warning for all the Clergy in York. Hear the word of the Lord oh You Blind Hipacrits you Saarpents and Vipears of Hell You Wine Bibears and beffe [beef] yeaters who Eyes Stand out with Fatness and still criing out mor Plum Pudding and Rost Beffe and Saying to your Souls Yeet and Drinke Soul and be meary.' The long letter was signed 'JM' and his Aldwark address was given.

A closer examination of his printed narrative revealed that Jonathan Martin had spent time in the lunatic asylums at West Auckland and Gateshead. He had been committed because of a bizarre incident that had occurred around the year 1817. Martin had told his wife that he intended to shoot the Bishop of Oxford with a pistol that he had borrowed from his brother. He left the pistol lying around as a test of faith. His wife sensibly removed it and since Martin 'received no encouragement from his dreams to proceed' he dropped the idea. However, someone informed against him to the magistrates who had him confined as insane.

Jonathan spent three years in Gateshead Asylum, and for the latter part of his incarceration he was restrained by leg-irons. Martin escaped by grinding the iron shackles with stones until one of them gave way. A trapdoor in the ceiling of his cell gave him access to the roof and he climbed down (Figure 2) and fled to the home of an uncle at Codley Hill near Hexham, where his leg-irons were filed off and he was given shelter, though the authorities do not appear to have searched for Martin in any serious way. After a period he seems to have slipped back into society quite openly. Indeed, the story of his escape was recounted in his pamphlet.

Many people were to testify that Martin's behaviour appeared perfectly rational except on one subject. He was a Wesleyan Methodist and like many Nonconformists in the nineteenth century he had a dislike of the set, formal prayers that formed the liturgy of the Church of England. Unfortunately his belief in spontaneous prayer from the heart grew into an obsession against the clergy, whom he believed were leading the higher ranks of society astray by their preaching and their way of life. This hatred of 'the blind guides'and 'the greedy wolves'became linked to persistent dreams that 'the son of Bonaparte'would surprise the unrepentant sinners and invade the country to 'be a scourge for the wicked clergymen of England'. His actions, attitude and extreme views resulted

Figure 2. Jonathan Martin's Providential Escape from the Asylum House. An engraving by Wm Martin in *The Life of Jonathan Martin.*

Figure 3. A Wanted Poster offering a reward for the capture of Jonathan Martin.

WHEREAS
JONATHAN MARTIN
'Stands Charged with having on the Night of the 1st of February, Instant,
WILFULLY SET FIRE TO
YORK
MINSTER.
A REWARD OF
100 *POUNDS*
Will be Paid on his being Apprehended and Lodged in any of his Majesty's Gaols.
And a Further Reward of
One Hundred Pounds
Will be paid on the Conviction of any ACCOMPLICES of the said JONATHAN MARTIN, to such Person or Persons as shall give Information which may lead to such Conviction.

The following is a Description of the said Jonathan Martin : viz.

He is rather a Stout Man, about Five Feet Six Inches high, with light Hair cut close, coming to a point in the centre of the Forehead, and high above the Temples, and has large bushy Red Whiskers ; he is between Forty and Fifty Years of Age, and of singular Manners. He usually wears a single-breasted blue Coat, with a stand-up Collar, and Buttons covered with the same cloth ; a black cloth Waistcoat ; and blue cloth Trowsers ; Half-Boots laced-up in front ; and a glazed, broad-brimmed, low-crowned Hat. Sometimes he wears a double-breasted blue Coat with yellow Buttons—When Travelling, he wears a large black leather Cape coming down to his Elbows, with two Pockets within the Cape ; there is a square piece of dark coloured Fur, extending from one shoulder point to the other—At other times he wears a drab coloured great Coat, with a large Cape and shortish Skirts—When seen at York last Sunday, he had on the double-breasted blue Coat, a common Hat, and his great Coat.

The said JONATHAN MARTIN is a Hawker of a Pamphlet entitled "The Life of Jonathan Martin, of Darlington, Tanner," the Third Edition of which is printed at Lincoln, by R. E. LEARY, 1829.—He had lodged in York about a Month, and quitted it on the 27th of January last, stating that he was going to Tadcaster for a few Days, and thence to Leeds. He returned to York on the 31st of January, and said that he and his Wife had taken Lodgings in Leeds. He was not seen in York after the 1st of February.

By Order of the DEAN and CHAPTER of YORK,
CHRIST. JNO. NEWSTEAD,
Clerk of the Peace for the Liberty of St. Peter of York.
York, 5th February, 1829.

BARNES & CO. PRINTERS, NORTH SHIELDS.

in Martin being excluded from Methodist Societies as a 'disturber of church services'.

A notice was issued in all the newspapers offering a description of Martin and a reward of one hundred pounds for his capture (Figure 3). There were also a number of posters put out.* The description read:

> *He is a rather stout man, about five feet six inches high, with light hair cut close, coming to a point in the centre of the forehead, and high above the temples, and has large bushy red whiskers; he is between forty and fifty years of age, and of singular manners. He usually wears a single-breasted blue coat, with a stand-up collar, and buttons covered with the same cloth; a black cloth waistcoat; and blue cloth trousers; half-boots laced up in front; and a glazed, broad-brimmed low-crowned hat (Figure 4). Sometimes he wears a double-breasted blue coat with yellow buttons. When travelling, he wears a large black cape coming down to his elbows, with two pockets within the cape; there is a square piece of dark coloured fur extending from one shoulder to the other. At other times he wears a drab coloured great coat, with a large cape and shortish skirts. When seen at York last Sunday, he had on the double-breasted blue coat, a common hat, and his great coat.*

Figure 4. A contemporary engraving showing Jonathan Martin in his famous cape and hat.

Following his attempt to burn down York Minster Jonathan Martin made no attempt at hiding his movements, and making his way back to his uncle's house Martin was arrested at 'Codlaw-hill, near Hexham'. He made no resistance and was brought back to York (Figure 5).

Whilst he was awaiting trial Martin continued to attract considerable attention (Figure 6). Considered a curiosity, the public were admitted to the goal to view him. He was under constant guard, however, even when sleeping in the hospital room at night. On the Friday before his court appearance, despite the presence of his guard asleep in the other bed in the room,

MARTIN
Apprehended.

Jonathan Martin,
Who stands charged with having set Fire to York Minster, on the Night of the 1st of February instant, was APPREHENDED near to Hexham, on FRIDAY, the 6th inst., and lodged in the House of Correction at that place.

CHRIS. JNO. NEWSTEAD,
Clerk of the Peace for the Liberty of St. Peter, York.
Residence, York, Saturday Morning, February 7, 1829, Half past Ten o'Clock.

H. Bellerby, Printer, Gazette-Office, York.

Figure 5. A poster printed in 1829, giving notice of the capture of Jonathan Martin.

Martin constructed nine yards of rope from the bed covers. Stripping to his shirt and drawers, he climbed up the chimney in the room, but was frustrated by an iron grating blocking any exit near the top. He managed, however, to return to his bed without waking the guard and, in the morning to wash the soot away in the yard without causing alarm, but the presence of soot in the room led to the discovery of his escape attempt.

Jonathan's trial was heard as part of the City Assizes in the Guildhall on 28 March. When the doors were opened at eight o'clock in the morning, there was a rush of spectators to get the best possible positions. Many of those present, it was noted, were well-dressed and highly respectable women. Martin had been brought to the court as early as six o'clock that day. He was delighted with the bustle, standing in the dock to make himself more visible to the crowd and talking and laughing with the press. He smiled complacently, claiming 'people made as much talk about him as Bonaparte'.

Figure 6. Jonathan Martin in York Prison. An engraving after a portrait by E. Lindley, 'taken in prison by permission of the Magistrates'.

Mr Justice Bayley had to enter the hall through the crowd. As he did so, a rush took place of the people still in the Guildhall Yard, so that it was only with great difficulty that a passage was kept free for the judge to reach his bench. Martin laughed at the scene. 'This is a very throng day', he said. 'They'll have the poor old man down.' It was perhaps the pressure from the crowd and the potential threat to public order that led Mr Sergeant Jones for the defence to rise and 'in a very low tone of voice'make an application for the removal of the case to the County Court at the Castle. The application was granted.

The trial at the County Assizes which took place on Monday, 31 March was equally well attended, and was presided over by Justice

Figure 7. Jonathan Martin as he appeared in his trial for setting fire to York Minster at the time the rope ladder was produced. From *A Report of the Trial of Jonathan Martin* (Baldwin & Craddock, 1829).

Baron Hullock. The east and west galleries, as well as the Grand Jury Box were reserved by courtesy of the High Sheriff for a fashionable audience of ladies and gentlemen. Martin spent the time waiting for proceedings to commence by hurriedly pacing about the floor of the dock with his arms folded. When the doors to the courtroom were thrown open to a tremendous surge of spectators, Martin jumped upon the bench in the dock and showed his delight (Figure 7). He had to be wrestled down into submission by the attending gaolers.

In the main, the trial hinged around two separate issues; was Martin the man responsible for the fire and, if so, what was his state of mind at the time? The prosecution spent some time outlining the law relating to insanity, stressing that it was the state of mind at the time the deed was carried out that mattered. If at that moment, the prisoner was capable of knowing good from evil, then he was answerable for his actions even if, at other times, he was unbalanced.

On one hand, the prosecution's case to show that Martin was responsible for the deed was simply a formality since Martin went out of his way to claim the deed as his own. He had kept the velvet, the gold fringe and the tassels from the Archbishop's throne to prove that he alone was responsible and so that no one else should take the blame or share the credit. He had left the pincers in a place of safety where they would be found so that they would be returned to the shoemaker, who could not afford to lose them. When he spoke for twenty minutes in his own defence, Martin rambled through an account of his dreams in which the Lord had chosen him to destroy York Minster 'for the wrong that was done by the clergy in going to plays and card tables and dinners'.

The rest of the trial was taken up largely by expert witnesses who had observed Jonathan Martin and were in a position to judge his sanity. Mr Caleb Williams, a surgeon who was retained by the Quakers'Retreat in York (Figure 8), the city's foremost mental institution, diagnosed him as a monomaniac, one whose insanity was confined to a single topic. Under cross-examination he explained that Martin could not distinguish between right and wrong on the subject of his delusion. He did not believe that the prisoner was feigning insanity. Dr Wake agreed. He had detected a wound in the frontal bone of Martin's skull, the result of an accident. The attempt to escape was not evidence that he knew right from wrong, merely that after a period of great excitement, a collapse of emotions takes place that is then followed by a period of lucidity. The cross-examination of the experts by the prosecution was half-hearted. There was an attempt to suggest that Martin was sane at the time of the fire, but it was obvious to all that they were merely going through the motions in challenging Martin's insanity.

The judge's summing up took one-and-a-half hours and he concentrated on the question of Martin's state of mind. He dwelt on the five letters written by Martin to the clergy as 'indicating a diseased understanding'. He pointed out that Jonathan Martin was not satisfying any personal injury by his act.

By contrast, the jury took only ten minutes to reach a verdict. The foreman declared, 'We find him guilty, but consider he was insane at the time he committed the act', but had to be corrected by the judge, who pointed out that that meant a 'not guilty'verdict! Martin was sent from York on 27 April 1829 to the Criminal Lunatic Asylum, St George's Fields, in London, the Hospital of St Mary of Bethlehem, popularly known as 'Bedlam, to be detained at His Majesty's pleasure.

Figure 8. A nineteenth century engraving of The Retreat.

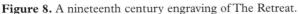

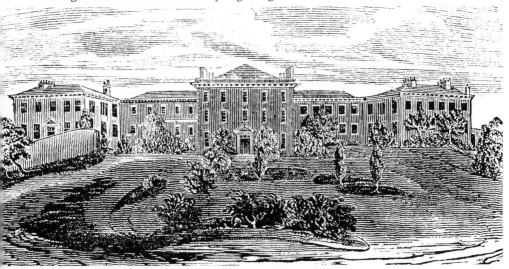

POTTERY MUG
MADE SOON AFTER
THE
BURNING
OF
YORK MINSTER
BY
JONATHAN MARTIN
ON
FEBY 2ND 1829.

Figure 9. Two postcards produced showing other souvenirs to mark the occasion of the fire at York Minster.

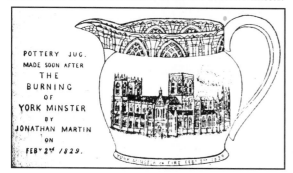

POTTERY JUG.
MADE SOON AFTER
THE
BURNING
OF
YORK MINSTER
BY
JONATHAN MARTIN
ON
FEBY 2ND 1829.

He was taken as far as Street House in a post-chaise, and then to the capital by express coach accompanied by an under-gaoler. Later, Martin was transferred to St Luke's Hospital, London, where he remained until his death on 27 May 1838 at the age of fifty-six or fifty-seven years old. Four days later his son Richard wrote an account of his last days to William Martin, who characteristically published it in a newspaper from which a cutting is pasted into the Bodleian Library's volume of William's pamphlets (198 e 76). His wife moved to Hull for a time and continued to sell the pamphlets *The Life of Jonathan Martin*, but charged a guinea a copy following the trial!

*Posters as illustrated are known to have been printed by H. Bellerby of York; Barnes & Co of North Shields; and J. Clark of Newcastle-upon-Tyne. It seems probable that the text was issued to a printer in each of the chief towns of Northumberland, Durham, and Yorkshire.

Sources

The Life of Jonathan Martin, of Darlington, Tanner, written by Himself. Darlington; Thomas Thompson, 1825.
ditto. Second Edition. Barnard Castle; Thomas Clifton, 1826.
ditto. Third Edition. Lincoln; R.E. Leary, 1828.
Report of the Trial of Jonathan Martin, etc. London; Baldwin & Cradock. York; Barclay, 1829. By arrangement with the solicitors for the prosecution and the defence, the publisher Barclay engaged Mr Fraser of Thavies Inn, London, to make a full short-hand report of the trial. The solicitors certify that it is the only full and authentic account. The appendix contains proofs of further evidence which, in order to shorten the case, was not produced at the trial.
A Full and Authentic Report of the Trial of Jonathan Martin, etc. York; Bellerby, 1829. Contains the fullest account of the fire, of the resultant damage, and of the public proceedings in York between the dates of the fire and the final trial.
The Life of Jonathan Martin, the Insane prophet and Incendiary. Barnard Castle; Thomas Clifton, nd [1829]. Reprints Jonathan's own Life and adds valuable accounts of the fire and subsequent proceedings. It gives the full text of the letters written by Matthew Wilson to the *Tyne Mercury.*
York Courant and Hull Advertiser 6 February 1829; 13 February 1829; 27 March 1829; 3 April 1829.
Hargrove's, *New Guide to the City of York,* 1838.
Balston, Thomas *The Life of Jonathan Martin Incendiary of York Minster with some account of William and Richard Martin.* MacMillan & Co. 1945.
Concise Dictionary of National Biography. Oxford University Press, 1992.
Article first published in part 1993 *Crimes and Punishments in Yorkshire 1800-1837* by Peter Howorth. Lowndes Publications, Driffield (01377 253768).

5. A Short History of the Bar Convent

by Sister Gregory Kirkus IBVM

THE BRASS PLATE on the front door, inscribed *The Bar Convent, 1686,* probably arouses no emotion in the visitor. But it should do so, because it is the title page of the epic history of the house. For the frontispiece of the story we must conjure up in our minds a picture of an elderly woman in a nondescript dress, putting her hand to a legal document. It may seem very ordinary, but everything about the scene is significant - the date, the place, the woman, her dress and her purpose.

The day is 5 November, not a very auspicious date for Catholics to embark on a new venture with the Gunpowder Plot still a vivid memory. The year is 1686, exactly one hundred and fifty years since King Henry VIII's commissioners destroyed religious life at the river side end of Nunnery Lane by expelling the nuns from Clementhorpe. These Benedictine sisters had been the centre of life in that hamlet. Their little chapel had a single bell that called the faithful to Mass and the community to its daily office. In their religious habits, the nuns were to be seen not only in choir, but mowing the hay in their meadow and gathering the apples in their orchard. Then in 1536 they disappeared, the chapel bell fell silent and the buildings gradually crumbled into ruins.

Now, in the year 1686, religious life returned at the other end of Nunnery Lane, but it returned in secret due to the penal laws of the times. The woman in our picture is signing the document with an assumed name, and she is not wearing religious dress.

She is Frances Bedingfield, a member of the distinguished, staunchly Catholic family of Bedingfield of Norfolk (Figure 1). She joined Mary Ward's Institute in 1632, and was present at her death-bed in 1645. With the other companions she left England for Paris and then in 1667, when already 'past the media of her age', she headed a small group of courageous women sent to make a permanent

Figure 1. Frances Bedingfield (1616-1704) the first Superior of the Bar Convent.

Figure 2. Sir Thomas Gascoigne (1596-1689) the founder of the Bar Convent.

foundation in England. Optimistically, they came in their religious habits and were promptly clapped in gaol. They emerged wiser, changing their habits for a 'matronly dress', later described as slate-coloured gowns and hoods. Frances adopted the alias of Frances Long, and with that name we see her signing the contract for a property on the site where the Convent now stands.

The penal laws of England were not the only obstacle between Frances and success. The Institute to which she belonged had been suppressed for ever in 1631; fortunately the Pope left a loop-hole by which it was able to continue a fragile existence, but it had no recognition by the Church and was allocated no duties within it; its members in the north lived in borrowed houses, with poverty as their constant companion. So the words of Sir Thomas Gascoigne (Figure 2), 'we must have a school for our daughters' were music in Frances Bedingfield's ear. They constitute the charter of the house, and the grand old man matched his words with a gift of £450, and part of that sum purchased a property there. An old print shows what appears to be two small houses joined together by a very plain, narrow porch (Figure 3).

If Frances had hoped to escape the vigilant eyes of the magistrates

Figure 3. The Bar Convent as it stood in 1686 when first purchased.

by choosing a modest property outside the city walls, she was disappointed, for the 'Ladies of the Bar' were soon the victims of the common informer. The house was frequently searched, vestments and other property impounded, and in 1694 Mother Frances and her great niece Dorothy were arrested by order of the Lord Mayor and committed to the horrible Ousebridge Gaol. From this 'loathsome prison' Frances wrote a letter to the Archbishop of York that is a model of courtesy, tact and dignity. Knowing him to be full of 'mercie and pitty' she begs him to use all his favour for the release of herself who 'want but two years of being eighty years old' and her companion. Mercifully their imprisonment was short, but worse was to follow. A few years later a fanatical mob made a formidable attack on the house, and all seemed lost. Placing themselves under the protection of St Michael, the sisters knelt in the entrance hall listening to the blows on the front door and expecting no mercy when the assailants broke in. The legend of St Michael appearing over the house on a white horse and with sword drawn may be a pious addition to the story but contemporary witnesses declared that 'no word of command was given, yet the mob suddenly became quiet and melted away'. So today an engraving of St Michael hangs over the front door, and his timely rescue of the house is commemorated annually on the eve of his feast.

In 1699 Frances Bedingfield, in her eighty-fourth year, was recalled to Germany. Her intended successor was Mother Mary Portington, described as having good judgement and 'preserving her patience in all calamities'; but a family lawsuit rendered it 'imprudent' for this desirable nun to be in the North of England, so it fell to Dorothy Bedingfield, alias Paston, to be the second Mother Superior of the Bar Convent. An examination of two portraits in the Great Parlour explain the misfortunes of Madame Paston, as she was commonly called. Frances appears bluff, hearty and self-confident, while Dorothy, whose picture hangs fittingly below that of her great-aunt, is seen as nervous, indecisive and perhaps lacking in personality. She was woefully unsuccessful in her office, and suffered the indignity of being the subject of letters of complaint written by members of the community to the General Superior. But she must not be unjustly belittled. Madame Paston stayed at her uncongenial post for thirty-four years and saw the house through a period of poverty so intense that at one time closure seemed inevitable. At the moment of crisis, however, Elizabeth Stanfield entered the noviceship. She was the only child of her parents and inherited a modest fortune that paid off the debts of the community and averted disaster. So in 1734 Madame Paston died solvent, but the future of the house was by no means assured.

A further danger occurred when Doctor Jaques Sterne, uncle of the novelist, presented himself at the convent. No visitor could have been less welcome. This greedy place-hunter was already Precentor of York Minster, a Canon Residentiary, Prebendary of York and Durham, and Rector of Rise and Hornsey-cum-Riston. He had received accolades for being a loyal Hanoverian during the '45 Rebellion and it appears he hoped to add to his string of benefices by making a foray against the Bar Convent.

Without explanation he insisted that the children be sent home and the community dispersed, threatening them with the full weight of the law if he was not obeyed. Many of the laws against Catholics were seldom enforced, but they were still on the statute book, and the nuns were badly shaken. At a final deliberation they were about to give in when Sister Eleonora Clifton stood up and said:

I have consecrated myself to the service of God to labour for the salvation of souls in this house and while a wall of it is still standing I will never leave it.

All took heart from her bold speech and resolved to stay. Dr Sterne was as bad as his word. Mother Hodshon and a companion were summoned before the Spiritual Court, charged with not receiving Holy Communion in Holy Trinity Church on one of the prescribed days. Providentially, the case was badly prepared and went by default because the indolent vicar had not held a service on that day. Strangely, the ill-natured Doctor Sterne later became the champion of the community he had persecuted and even offered to fight its battles!

This incident was the last serious attack made on the Convent, and now we may address the question, how did they live? This group of women, some ten or twelve in number, small in stature (to judge by the low lintels and short chair-legs) but robust in spirit, what was their daily life? Frugality and charity are the key words to the answer. Frugality was imposed upon them by the persistent poverty that accompanied them day after day, year after year. The school was small and the nuns had to eke out a livelihood by keeping hens, pigs, sheep and a white cow. The economies practised are recorded in a black exercise book kept by Mother Davies the 'procuratrix' or housekeeper. This artless book details the re-bottoming of the nuns' chairs and beds with sackcloth, the shelf made out of an old cheese board, the old gowns converted into bed covers, the re-tinning of pans and the re-use of candle ends. Even so, the bottom line of many pages in the monthly account book reads, 'spent above ye income'. Financial security was an unknown luxury.

Intimate as are Mother Davies' entries, we learn more about the sisters' daily life in the eighteenth century from another manuscript book entitled 'Rules of Office'. As we turn the pages the office-holders spring into action and perform their tasks, so that we watch the daily round of the community acted out like a peep-show before our eyes. The 'caller-up' 'rises at least a quarter of an hour before the rest' and taking her lantern makes the round of the dark corridors, rousing the sleepers and lighting their candles. The charity that pervades the day is exercised even in this dreary hour before dawn, for those who do not get up when called - and how human it is to find some still abed! - are dubbed 'the slow risers'. The cook is also up betimes, lighting the kitchen fire, but 'not using more wood than is needful,' preparing the meals punctually and being careful to use a fork and not touch the food with her fingers. Then, when the teachers have gone to the classrooms, the Buyer sallies forth to do the shopping, the Portress guards the door and admits externs with caution, the Keeper of Garments and the Keeper of Linen ply their needles for the benefit of the household and the Prefect of Books makes sure that 'all the books are rankt and in due order, those of a kind together.' There seems to be an office for everyone and the house is a hive of activity.

The duties of the Infirmarian are arduous. She must make the beds 'decently', keep the infirmary clean and tidy, stoke up the fire, provide well-dressed food and carry out the orders of the 'phisisian' [physician]. Further, she must cheer the patients with words of comfort and little gifts. Finally, she is urged to bear with patience the troubles and difficulties of attending the sick.

Meanwhile the teachers are in the classroom trying to obey the lofty precepts laid down for them. They are to have a 'humble bearing', to 'avoid hastiness of speech with sharp and biting words' but rather 'admonish in a spirit of mildness'. They are to have no favourites, but a 'general propension and affection must be shown toward all.' For the actual teaching, the golden rule of pedagogy is expressed quaintly but clearly, the teacher

> ...*must observe the wit and capacity of everyone in particular and so accommodate her instructions to the measure of their under-standing that those who are advanced may advance further and those who are more backwards be not neglected.*

The Mother Superior is vested with overall authority but, like the rest, she too is subject to the rules of office and charity. 'Let her utmost endeavour make it her particular business to comfort any in their afflictions and to excite the tepid and slothful.' She must see 'that she supplies everyone with the proper remedies according as their distempers or infirmities requisites.'

Finally, a little vignette shows the sisters on a journey. On the road they must 'endeavour by frequent prayers to deserve that Christ may accompany them', and if they travel on foot they 'must let the weaker go foremost, and by the measure of their strength and ability they must regulate their stages; and if any happen to fall by the way they must provide for her, not regarding her person but the necessity of the circumstances and what true charity requires.'

This spirit of charity was put into execution outside the community as well as within it. The 'Ladies of the Bar' visited the sick and Sister Eleonora ran what we should call today a clinic in the little porch of the old house. Here the local people came with their ailments, receiving treatment and sympathy. So gifted was Sister Eleonora that she once saved the leg of a young man who had met with a terrible accident, and in his gratitude he offered her his hand in marriage. Unable to explain that she was a nun, the sister could only reply courteously, 'I thank you, sir, but I am already engaged'.

Death came at last to all members of the community, often sooner, rather than later, for short lives were not uncommon. The law was harsh to Catholics both living and dead, and they could be refused burial in consecrated ground held by Anglicans. Yet the eighteenth century incumbents of Holy Trinity church, in Micklegate, were charitable, tolerant or indifferent and so from 1734 to 1826 the bodies of the nuns were taken discreetly at dusk, to be buried with decent but minimal ceremony in a corner of the churchyard, where their nameless grave-slabs can still be seen.

The purpose of the Bar Convent foundation was to provide a school, in accordance with Mary Ward's aims for well-educated women and to fulfil the conditions laid down by Thomas Gascoigne. As a consequence, the school was the main thrust of the community, offering education to the daughters of the hunted recusant gentry. An examination of the list of pupils admitted between the years 1710 and 1800 shows that all the prominent recusant families were represented, as in a roll of honour. Here can be found the daughters of Bedingfield, Clifford, Constable, Lawson, Scrope, Stourton, Stapleton, Tempest, Towneley, Vavasour and Weld, families all scarred by persecution. A more careful scrutiny, however, reveals the presence of a middle-class element from quite an early date. With the admission of the Humbles from Newcastle, the Hobsons of

Pontefract, the Waltons of Manchester and the Smelters of Sheffield, it is clear that coal-mining, the iron industry and 'King Cotton' claimed places in the school. It was an age, too, of colonisation and commercial enterprise; the Liverpool merchants grew rich and though their families lacked distinction they had social ambitions and the money to pay school fees. As the century wore on the spread of the commercial empire is reflected in the presence of English girls from the trading posts of Cadiz and Barcelona, the West Indies, Allahabad and Calcutta.

This situation prompts the question: in such a class-conscious age, did the daughters from Hazlewood Castle, Broughton Hall and Rudding Park sit happily in the classroom with girls from very different social backgrounds, who spoke with northern accents? We shall probably never know the whole truth, but a clue might be read into an entry in the Convent *Journal* dated 20 October 1775 that states:

> *Mr Humble came to fetch his daughter who against her will leaves us, but is resolved to come again to us if possible.*

So at least one child of the Industrial Revolution, a collier's daughter, was happy at school with members of the old aristocracy.

Sadly we know little about the school curriculum. Very few text-books have survived, but the eighteenth century library books suggest a general fluency in modern languages. Not much more is to be learnt from the 'Young Ladies' bills, extant from 1761. Dancing, at two guineas a term, was an almost universal extra, while drawing (taught by Mr Joseph Halfpenny) and music must have been included in the basic school fees as they appear on the bills only as charges for materials and the hire of instruments.

While the bills are short on pedagogy they are a rich source of information about school life. Holidays were spent at the Bar Convent until the coming of the railways, so the nuns had to act in *loco parentis*. The bills are thus full of homely items such as cotton and worsted stockings, gloves and mitts, the 'amending' of shoes and stays, and the 'letting out' of other garments. With a closer inspection we make the cheerful discovery that school life was far from gloomy and that the nuns were anything but killjoys. Piecing together the materials, ornaments and clothes mentioned, we have a picture of the 'misses' looking very smart when they went out in their gaily-coloured cloaks, silk hats, ruffles, ribands and ear-rings. There were celebrations for birthdays, with special fare for the child in question and all her friends. The item 'hire of chair' must refer to a sedan chair, which perhaps took two of the older girls to a concert in the

Assembly Rooms, and coach fare suggests the occasional visit home, perhaps for a wedding or christening in the family.

Further details can be gleaned from Mother Davies' black log-book; she must have been a kindly person and very fond of the children for not only did she make sure, very properly, that they had better furniture and more amenities than the nuns, but she provided 'a swing for the misses to rock in', also a cribbage set, a fox-and-geese board, a book of robberies and a copy of Robinson Crusoe (which begins, you remember, with the words 'I was born in the City of York)'. She took them to St Luke's Fair and gave them 'spending money' to have fun with while she hunted for bargains and came away with Delpht porringers, tea-cups with handles, and a mousetrap. There must have been a Nativity Play at Christmas, perhaps produced by Mother Davies, for she provided 'a bag for the King's hair' and crooks for the shepherds.

There were sad as well as happy times, and a tragic story is related in a single page of the *Young Ladies' Account Book*. Mary Clifton appears in the first few lines as a normal child who has cambric for her ruffles, pomatom for her hair and a scarlet cloak. Half-way down the page the items 'a fire in her bed-chamber and chocolate, sugar and biscuits' suggests the need for special care. The situation becomes more grave when a nurse has to be hired and there are charges for a doctor, a surgeon, and an apothecary. Evidently their efforts were of no avail for the next items are 'a coffin, candles, a fine crepe burial suite, underbearers and a velvet pall' and the sad story ends with 'wine and biskets at the funeral.' Between the lines of the conventional bill we read of the anxiety and the grief, and our imagination pictures the sorrowful funeral cortege passing under Micklegate Bar on its short journal to Holy Trinity churchyard.

Though the sources that tell of everyday life are still not exhausted we must pass on to record the all-important reconstruction of the property, above all, the building of the Chapel. Here we meet the great figure of Mother Ann Aspinal, a Lancashire woman, born in 1710 and educated at the Bar Convent (Figure 4). She entered the novitiate at the age of seventeen and spent thirty busy years occupying almost every office in the house. In 1760 she became the Mother Superior and embarked upon a further

Figure 4. Ann Aspinal (1710-89), Superior of the Bar Convent who was responsible for the building of the Chapel.

twenty-nine years of activity that totally transformed the Bar Convent premises. Her portrait shows a woman at once sensitive, shrewd and determined. With great business acumen Mother Aspinal settled the finances of the house on a firm footing, writing to the General Superior:

> *At the close of this year* [1766] *I have found the accounts very satisfactory.*

The following year she reported:

> *I have the consolation of telling you that since I knew this house, the school has never flourished as it does now.*

With forty fee-paying pupils and the modest support of her friends, Mother Aspinal began to build. The *Journal* gives brief but vivid details. 'The garden wall broke down at the corners,' runs one entry, 'and two large gates put up to let in the carriages which brought in materials for the building, bricks, lime, wood, etc'. Then on 24 February 1766, 'the old house was begun to be pulled down and we removed to Mrs Smith's house which was taken for two years.' The rent was twenty-six pounds per annum. The foundation stone for the new house was laid on 4 March and the whole was covered in by 3 December of the following year.

Foremost in Ann Aspinal's plans was the building of a chapel (Figure 5). She chose as her architect Thomas Atkinson, who had recently designed neo-Gothic additions to Bishopthorpe Palace. One may conjecture that when invited to the Bar Convent he thought he would further exploit the latest fashion and build the nuns 'a nice little Gothic chapel.' But his client had other ideas. Mother Aspinal had obtained details of a church 'outside Rome' (possibly Santa Constanza) and was determined to imitate its style. In the event the plans had to be modified to accommodate a situation of penal laws and hostile public opinion. Eventually the Chapel was placed within the building complex, overlooking not the street but an enclosed garden. There is nothing ecclesiastical about its windows,

Figure 5. The Bar Convent Chapel, built to a design by Thomas Atkinson (d. 1798).

Figure 6. A nineteenth century engraving of the Bar Convent before Andrews, 1845 addition to the corner of Nunnery Lane.

and the dome, which in Italy would have been a dominant feature, was brought low and covered with a slate roof. Thus there was no outward appearance of a Chapel to inflame the anger of a fanatical mob. One of the laws still in effect at that date was the prohibition to hear or say Mass, and informers were plying a lucrative business, so the Chapel was provided with eight exits, to allow the congregation plenty of escape routes, should pursuivants make a surprise visit. For the safety of the celebrant a priest's hiding-hole was constructed under the floor.

The annals of the Bar Convent have surprisingly little to say about the building of this neo-classical gem, but in a letter dated 1767, Ann Aspinal gives vent to a justifiable burst of pride when she wrote:

> *Our chapel is not yet finished. It is said that when completed it will be the handsomest and most commodious in these parts.*

She spoke of saying her *Nunc Dimittis* when the chapel was opened. Not content with her achievements, this stout-hearted woman went on to complete the Convent by erecting what the licence laconically called 'a new front wall to her house' - but which in actual fact was the building of the entire Georgian façade and the rooms immediately behind it (Figure 6). Mother Aspinal died at the age of seventy-nine and was interred in the chancel of Holy Trinity Church. Nothing marks her grave, but her monument is the Chapel and this house.

After years of struggle an evening glow shines over the convent in the last decade of the eighteenth century, and in this light the community - itself now free from persecution - is seen using its energy to serve the stream of refugees fleeing from the French Revolution. French girls came as pupils and hospitality was given to the impetuous Countess de Guyon Beaufort, who left her native shores with her two daughters in such haste that the community had to supply them with winter clothing. Such charitable actions, however, were not enough for Mother Catherine Rouby. At the height of the persecution she would send out her 'spies' or friends daily to watch the London coach come into Coney Street. Any French passengers, however disguised, were assumed to be nuns or priests and were directed to the Bar Convent where a warm welcome awaited them. Three communities of nuns (Carmelites, Poor Clares, and Canonesses of the Holy Sepulchre) were given shelter until new homes could be provided for them. For the priests Mother Rouby found lodgings in the city, and often employment as well. The refugees had sad stories to tell, and events brought tragedy into the very community itself.

Louise de Guyon Beaufort had already entered the noviceship when she heard of her father's execution. A few months later her mother, rashly heeding reports that the Revolution was over, returned to France with her other daughter. Not long afterwards Louise heard that her mother, sister and brother had all perished on the guillotine. A little French book of devotion in the library bears the signature of Louise and is a poignant reminder of the horrors of that period overseas and of Mother Rouby's charity to those in need.

With the death of Mother Rouby in 1810 a new and somewhat pedestrian era set in. Elizabeth Coyney, the next Mother Superior, was an unfortunate woman who has been blamed for calamities that were in part beyond her control. Soon after coming into office she heard that the Papal Bull *Quamvis Justo* denied Mary Ward the title of foundress. Dismayed at her past veneration of Mary as such, in reparation she destroyed every trace of Mary Ward in the house - pictures, letters, books and memorabilia perished in the ensuing holocaust.

A second course of action was equally serious. During the Napoleonic War communication broke down between York and the continent. Receiving no answer from her letters, Mother Coyney feared that the Institute had been suppressed; and when a priest friend, disguised as a peddler, brought news that the nuns had been expelled from the *Paradeiserhaus* in Munich, she concluded, erroneously, that the Institute had not survived. Acting in good faith, she placed the Bar Convent under the authority of the Bishop, and at the same time the community took the decision to observe strict enclosure. Both steps were contrary to the wishes of Mary Ward and were to have dire consequences.

Mother Coyney timidly resisted suggestion for a new foundation. The parish priest of Leeds, Father Underhill, prevailed upon her to make the journey there, but relates the annalist sadly, 'the affair ended with that day's drive.' Nevertheless, she unwittingly set on foot a much greater expansion when in the year 1813 she received into the noviceship Mary Aikenhead and Alicia Walsh, two young Irish women destined by Archbishop Murray, of Dublin, to found the Irish Sisters of Charity. In 1814, they were joined by a third novice, Frances Ball who, after her formation, also returned to Dublin and founded the Loreto branch of the Institute. Thus the Bar Convent fostered two world-wide religious orders. At home, Mother Coyney is to be remembered for laying down the cemetery as a safeguard against the activities of the 'Resurrection men'. She died in 1826 and was the first nun to be buried there.

Throughout the nineteenth century progress and prosperity were

Figure 7. The Bar Convent as it is today showing the alterations by G.T. Andrews in 1845. Compare this picture with Figure 6.

Figure 8. The Bar Convent entrance Hall. *From a drawing by Bridget Tempest.*

expressed in terms of bricks and mortar as further accommodation was provided for both school and community. Most noticeable (and regrettable) is the 1845 addition at the corner of Nunnery Lane, designed by G.T. Andrews. With its pretentious pilasters and heavy pediment, it is an unworthy neighbour to the Georgian façade, but it is remarkable for its large stone cross surmounting the roof (Figure 7). This was the first outward sign of the religious function of the property, and so stands for a symbol of Catholic emancipation. It was the same G.T. Andrews who glazed the central courtyard, using iron ties that betray his profession as a railway architect. The floor was then laid with encaustic Maw tiles and, with the addition of early ironwork benches, the front hall assumed its present Victorian appearance (Figure 8).

The Industrial Revolution impinged upon every aspect of life in the house. The community invested its growing savings in the railways, and reaped sufficient reward to provide central heating in the Chapel at a cost of thirty-four pounds and a domestic heating system that obviated the necessity of journeys to Fulford for baths. With the coming of the railways, summer holidays at home were introduced for the pupils. These were first described as an 'indulgence', with no allowance on the bill, but they soon became part of the curriculum.

Education remained at the heart of the apostolate, and the nineteenth century fee sheets reveal the wide range of modern languages, musical skills and other accomplishments offered to equip the girls for their station in life. But while the 'young ladies' were busy acquiring French, Italian and German, mastering the harp and enjoying their beadwork, Mother Angela Browne was introducing her community to new spheres of educational activity. By the middle of the century the Walmgate area of the city was full of immigrant Irish families, and to meet their needs St George's Church and School were erected. Mother Angela made financial contributions and dispatched two nuns, by cab, to teach in the school. They were furnished with rules to ensure strict decorum in the classroom, but upon arrival found themselves faced with 'a crowd of wild-looking little creatures squalid and dirty, shouting and screaming.' For over ten years the sisters laboured in the school under difficult conditions of overcrowded classrooms, smoky stoves and an almost total lack of equipment. Even when they were withdrawn, Mother Angela continued to present the prizes at the school, and to entertain the children to an annual tea-party in the Convent garden.

In 1858 she ventured further afield, accepting an invitation to establish a house in Scarborough. The 'Middle School' was short-lived but a Poor School and night-classes for working girls were well-established when Bishop Briggs died and was succeeded by Robert Cornthwaite. Hitherto the community had not suffered from the direct rule of the Bishop, for John Briggs was a kindly, genial Father Superior and everybody's favourite. By contrast, his heavy-handed successor arrived with a prejudice against the Bar Convent and, full of reforming zeal, he set forth on a Visitation that lasted eight months and was to change every detail of the sisters' lives, even forbidding them to have baths unless so prescribed by the doctor. He disapproved of what he called 'branch houses' and insisted on withdrawal from Scarborough. The community begged that the Convent should be retained for the use of old and sick members, but the Bishop was adamant. 'He thought that the nuns should wait till they got to heaven for a change of air,' wrote the annalist.

However, this formidable prelate gave his full support to a more important project. The Institute, widespread and flourishing, remained under the official ban of 1631, and repeated attempts to win Papal recognition had all failed. In 1876 Mother Julianna Martin, encouraged by Father John Morris, SJ, resolved to make a further appeal. Backed by the full weight of episcopal authority and supported by the Loreto Sisters, she dispatched her petition to Rome. With surprisingly little delay Pope Pius IX issued a *Decree of Approbation* on 4 February 1877. As a consequence, a small community isolated from the mainstream of the Institute and temporarily in schism from the General Superior achieved what cardinals, priests and princes of great authority and influence had failed to achieve.

Despite this flash of glory there was a dark side to the contemporary community life. Reading the annals, rules and customs book, one misses the robust spirit of courage and enterprise that prevailed in the previous century. Security may have had a debilitating effect and certainly enclosure took its toll; for what sort of apostles could be formed by rules that forbade the inmates to look out of the windows facing the street and bade them try not to think of events outside the Convent walls? Small wonder that the *Customs Book* is more concerned with the minute details about laying the tables than with the Greater Glory of God. The result of this impoverishment of spirit was a joyless religious life; and so out of the eighty-three young women who entered the novitiate between 1850 and 1900, thirty-nine left the Convent, some after only a few week's trial. Fortunately the rule of enclosure weakened towards 1900, and another sign of grace was the renewal of devotion to Mary Ward.

At the turn of the nineteenth century the Superior was Mother Frances Pope, whose genial features, winningly caught by the portrait painter, express the optimism of a new age. It was she who sent five nuns to Cambridge in 1898, to make what eventually became a successful foundation there. She also played her part in the struggle to regain for Mary Ward her rightful title of foundress of the Institute, and it must have been Mother Frances that received the telegram from Rome that announced victory with the words, 'Foundress recognized by Pope'.

There followed a general movement for unity, and in 1911 the communities of York and Cambridge recognised the authority of the General Superior. Bishop William Gordon graciously resigned his claim to be Superior of the house, and it returned to the mainstream Institute.

In the twentieth century the community contributed to the efforts of the Great War of 1914-18 by giving hospitality to Belgian refugee children and by turning the school hall into a ward for convalescent soldiers. The Second World War brought the tragedy of a direct hit on the house by enemy bombs and the death of five sisters.

In the school, revolutionary changes took place. The day and boarding schools were amalgamated in 1921 to form a Grammar School that won direct grant status. But in 1985, after some twenty years of discussion, York adopted the comprehensive system and it was agreed that the three Catholic schools in the city should form a single comprehensive establishment. Consequently, after nearly three hundred years the nuns relinquished their control and the Bar Convent school became part of All Saints Comprehensive.

Following this decision, the Georgian property became redundant and it was necessary to utilise the accommodation fittingly and at the same time generate some income for its upkeep. A museum was set up and acclaimed as a model of its kind, but proved a financial drain. During the Balkan War, Bosnian refugee children were accepted and liberally entertained, but success evaded every attempt to put the house to profitable use. In 1994 the Convent had to admit to its debts, sell its valuable Le Sueur painting and close for a year to decide its future.

Then at last drastic measures were taken. The whole building was radically altered to provide modern bed and breakfast accommodation, the lecture room was updated with the latest equipment and the old kitchens were re-decorated beyond recognition to create two more conference rooms. A business manager was appointed and soon viability, if not prosperity, was in sight. Thus the oldest Convent in England was saved from sale or demolition.

6. Bronze Plaque Guide to York

by Alan Whitworth

IN THE CITY OF YORK, history literally surrounds the visitor and resident alike; underfoot, overhead, in the very fabric of the buildings themselves. For nearly two thousand years 'great' events have unfolded here - war, famine, pestilence, joy and celebration - all of which, added up, have produced one of the most interesting and historic of English cities. Yet how much could have gone unobserved, unnoticed? Undoubtedly, it was partly with this in mind that the York Civic Trust rose to the challenge of illuminating and marking the kaleidoscope of events which have helped to make up the story of York when they instigated a programme of placing informative plaques around the walls, streets and buildings of this 'northern' capital.

The story of the Bronze Plaques is almost a story of the history of York Civic Trust itself, for both saw birth together - over fifty years ago and over one hundred plaques earlier. The York Civic Trust 'came into being' at a meeting held at the Mansion House on Thursday 18 July 1946 (Figure 1).

It was the City Corporation who originally proposed the idea of siting commemorative plaques on features of historic interest. Unfortunately, before the scheme could be taken up, Second World

Figure 1. A nineteenth century engraving of the Mansion House.

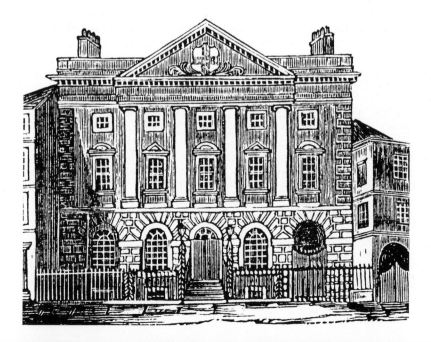

War broke out and the plan had to be dropped. After the hostilities, however, a revival of the idea was suggested by the York Civic Trust, and in 1946, the year of its formation, a small sub-committee was appointed to prepare a list of 'claimants to the honour' and to consider the most desirable types of material, form and lettering.

By 1947 their report was ready, and the sub-committee issued drawings and a proposed layout and lettering for the Judge's Lodgings, and suggested a further nine sites in the first instance to the estates Committee of the York Corporation. The plaques were to cost a total of £100, towards which the Trust would contribute a quarter. So enthusiastic was their commitment to getting the scheme re-introduced, that they had a trial piece designed and handmade in bronze and enamel by a Mr Syme. Sadly, however, it was another three years before any further progress of sorts was seen.

The annual report of the York Civic Trust for 1950-51 records that 'the designs have been obtained and approved, but jumps in the price of metals, and finally the embargo upon their use, have changed the situation adversely at almost every meeting of our Executive. The work is now being carried out by the Birmingham Guild'. At this time it was proposed to commemorate 'sites connected with John Wesley's sojourns in York' .

Regardless of setbacks, by the beginning of 1952 the scheme was up and running, and six plaques were 'evident in the streets to those who care to look for them' and these commemorated John Wesley, John Stanley Purvis, John Goodricke, and the Assembly Rooms. The Trust also 'consented to share costs with the Architectural and Archaeological Society in providing a plaque for the Roman Wall in St Leonard' s - just behind the bus stops.'

Since that year, practically every major historic event and

Figure 2. Bronze plaque affixed to the City walls in the nineteenth century.

personage who has served York has been 'commemorated' on a plaque. There are now nearly 150 plaques throughout the city, though not all have been set up by the York Civic Trust. Indeed, it is a credit to their efforts, however, that many others have been provided at the expense of individuals and companies in emulation and as a continuation of the scheme (Figure 2).

In 1979 the annual report emphasised the usefulness and value of these plaques, which was best expressed in a letter received from a visitor to York by the Town Clerk:- 'I would like to say how very much I appreciate the information boards attached to many places of interest in the City. They add much to one's pleasure; so satisfying to know some accurate facts about what you are looking at. The other thing that struck me was the really clear and pleasing script used on the boards.'

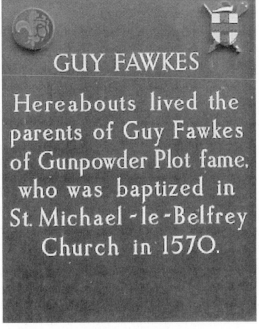

Figure 3. The York Civic Trust bronze plaque commemorating Guy Fawkes.

Latterly, the production of many of these bronze plaques was undertaken by Messrs J.R. Pearson Limited of Birmingham, but as costs, and indeed, interest escalated, and the amount of information required on each individual plaque increased, it became necessary to produce a number in other materials to suit varying situations. Larger boards, containing lengthy descriptions are often sign-written in the traditional manner in a distinctive green and gold livery (by Messrs Bellerby's) while others, often in pavement locations, have been cut in stone. There are a few cast-iron plaques, but, as the York Civic Trust annual report for 1978-79 points out, 'Most of the plaques are in bronze, and the cost of many of them has been shared with the Corporation. Done to a high standard of material, design, and historical accuracy, they are now recognised as invaluable guides to the City bringing history to life' (Figure 3).

One element that all the York Civic Trust plaques and boards

contain, however, is a distinctive motif (Figure 4). This is based on the York Assay mark which was ordained by statute in 1423, and which was before a change in 1698, half a fleur-de-lis and a half crowned lion's head divided per pale in a circle.

Finally, the scope of this publication does not permit the listing of all the plaques around York's streets, however, to serve as an example of style and the broad range of events and personalities covered I have reproduced one or two.

Figure 4. The motif of York Civic Trust which is placed on most plaques associated with them.

The first plaque erected was that on the railings of the Judges Lodgings, in Lendal. At the time it was put up the building was in use as the residence of the Judge. But later with its closure and eventual conversion to a hotel, the original plaque was removed and replaced with the following which differs from the first only in a slight change to the second from last line and the addition of the last line of text:

Judge's Lodgings. Built circa 1720 by Dr C.Winteringham (1689-1748) on the site of the Churchyard of St Wilfrid's Church. From 1806-1979 it was the official residence of HM Judges of Assize. It is now a hotel.

Another early plaque was that on the property 49 Bootham which records:

Joseph Rowntree 1836-1925. In this house lived a man whose life was to exercise a profound influence upon a City of which he became in 1911 an Honorary Freeman. A pioneer of research and reform in social policy and industrial relations, he became Chairman of the Company which bears his name and established three Trusts which seek to continue his work through the generous resources he gave to them.

Nearby, at No.33 another plaque commemorates another celebrity of the city:

Dr William Arthur Evelyn 1860-1935. A pioneer of the conservation of the City of York between 1891 and 1935, he lived in this house from 1910 to 1931. This plaque was erected by York Civic Trust and the Yorkshire Architectural and York Archaeological Society in 1985 to

Figure 5. A Hansom Cab invented by Joseph Aloysius Hansom, seen here in the streets of the York Castle Museum.

mark the 50th anniversary of his death.

Later, plaques often came to commemorate more modern events, as in these two instances which are associated with the royal family. The second plaque stands in the Museum Gardens while the first is situated in Minster Yard on the path leading to St William's College, and reads:

The Queen's path. Her Majesty Queen Elizabeth II walked from the West Door of the Minster along this way to the Treasurer's House after she distributed the Royal Maundy [Money] on March 30th 1972 .

This Observatory was built by the Yorkshire Philosophical Society following the inaugural meeting of the British Association for the Advancement of Science in 1831. It has an earlier rotating roof, designed by John Smeaton, who also designed the Eddystone Lighthouse. The Observatory housed what was for many years the largest refracting telescope in the world, designed and built by Thomas Cooke of York, whose firm also built the Greenwich transit instrument. It was restored and refitted to mark the British Association's anniversary meeting in York in 1981, and was officially

Figure 6. One of three York Civic Trust bronze plaques commemorating various aspects of the life of George Hudson.

opened by its President, The Duke of Kent, GCMG, GCVO.

Of course, with the passage of time itself, it is inevitable there will be changes, some losses. There is a note that in 1978 a replacement plaque was provided for 'one of the earliest', commemorating John Goodricke, which was stolen from its site on the railings of the Treasurer's House, in the Minster Yard. Interestingly, the replacement plaque, put up in the Silver Jubilee Year of Queen Elizabeth II, cost £600, the original, only £24!

In general, however, the majority of bronze plaques have remained in situ, and since the time I first began recording the plaques, of which a full list was published in a small booklet entitled, *The Bronze Plaque Guide to York,* only one that I noted has totally disappeared.

That this plaque once existed is proved by a brief note in the archives of the York Civic Trust and a mention in the 1973-74 statement of accounts of that society. Recording the man, Joseph Aloysius Hansom, responsible among other things for the invention and introduction of the 'Hansom Cab' (Figure 5), it was affixed to a building in Micklegate in 1970. However, since that time when I first noticed it in the 1980s, it has now gone. Other than that example, to my knowledge all others remain and tracking them around the streets is a fascinating way of spending a sunny afternoon and an excellent way of becoming acquainted with the city of York.

7. IN THE STEPS OF ST MARGARET CLITHEROW

by the late Katharine M. Longley

MARGARET CLITHEROW WAS BORN Margaret Middleton in York about the year 1553 in a house on the south-west side of Davygate, in the parish of St Martin, Coney Street, where she was baptised. Her parents were Thomas Middleton, a wealthy wax chandler, and his wife, Jane, whose maiden name was Turner (Figure 1).

Jane Turner's father, Richard, was the proprietor of the *Angel Inn*, in Bootham, situated on the north-east side of the street, fairly close to Bootham Bar. Both Richard Turner, who died in 1534, and his wife Margaret, after whom the future martyr was doubtless named, and who died in 1540, were buried in their parish church of St Olave's, in Marygate, before the altar of Saint Anne.

Their daughter Jane married Thomas Middleton in 1532, two years after his admission to the freedom of the city. In 1552 he was chosen to be one of the city

Figure 1. A contemporary likeness of Margaret Clitherow.

chamberlains, and in 1564 one of the two city sheriffs. From 1555 to 1558, as one of the four churchwardens of St Martin's he was responsible for continuing the restoration of the church for Catholic rites and practices, repainting and setting up the rood, repairing the Easter Sepulchre and making a cover for the newly restored high altar; he lived to see nearly all his work undone at the accession of Queen Elizabeth I.

In May 1567 Thomas Middleton died; he was buried in St Martin's Church in the middle aisle 'before the high choir'. Four months later, in the same church, his widow married a young Protestant from the south of England, Henry May. He proceeded to turn the family home in Davygate into an inn, and to build up an estate extending by the time of his death in 1596, as far as Coney Street, and north-west into the parish of St Helen, Stonegate.

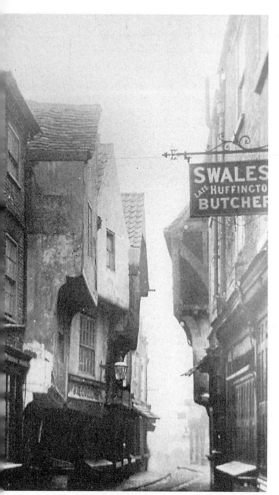

Figure 2. A nineteenth century photograph of the Shambles, the street of butchers.

Assisted by his wife's wealth he rose rapidly through the hierarchy of civic offices, becoming Lord Mayor of York in 1586, the year of his stepdaughter's death. His name may be read to this day on York City's Sword of State.

On 1 July 1571 Margaret Middleton, aged fifteen years, married a butcher, John Clitherow, in the church of St Martin, and removed to his house in the Shambles (Figure 2). Extensive research has identified this house, which until 1938 belonged to the Dean and Chapter of York, with the present property numbered 10 and 11 on the east side of the street. The property had been divided into two by 1731, and the fronts were rebuilt in brick some years before 1847. In no.10 the sculptor Robert Brumby, fired his statue of the Madonna and Child now in the Metropolitan Cathedral of Christ the King, in Liverpool.

John Clitherow had also inherited from his father an estate at Cornborough, a few miles to the north of York, lying on the north-east side of the River Foss. Though he kept servants there to tend to his sheep, it is known that he rarely stayed at the house; but his estate would have been very familiar to his wife, Margaret.

The house in the Shambles lay in the parish of Holy Trinity, King's Court, commonly known as Christ Church. The church, briefly attended by Margaret Clitherow from 1571 until about 1573, was finally demolished in 1937. Three of its bells, cast in about the year 1450 were presented in 1974 by the Rector and the Parish Council of All Saints, Pavement, through the good offices of the York Diocesan Committee for the Care of Churches, to the Carmelite

Fathers, then at Hazlewood Castle, near Tadcaster. Strangely enough, two of these bells already bore the names of Margaret and John.

The southern end of the Shambles runs into the Pavement where the market was normally held for the sale of butter, cheese, eggs, and poultry (Figure 3). It was here, at three o'clock in the afternoon of Friday, 22 August 1572, on a specially erected scaffold, that Thomas Percy, seventh Earl of Northumberland, one of the two leaders of the Catholic Rebellion of 1569, was beheaded. His public profession of faith was perhaps the first incident that turned Margaret's thoughts toward embracing the Catholic Church with which she was reconciled in 1574.

By this date her husband John had been chosen to assist the churchwardens of Christ Church in reporting 'recusants', those who for reasons of conscience refused to attend their parish church. Now his wife was one of these.

It is not known how Margaret obtained instruction in the Catholic faith, but it may have been through Dorothy Vavasour, wife of Dr Thomas Vavasour. She ran a Catholic 'maternity home' where mothers 'had good and safe being, both for the time of their delivery, the christening of their children, and the recovery of their health again'. There was frequently a priest hidden in the Vavasour's house, which at this period was situated on the north-east side of Ogleforth,

Figure 3. All Saints' Church, Pavement and the old Butter Cross and on the right the demolished church of St Crux which stood at one end of the Shambles.

close to its junction with Chapter House Street. From 1576, however, Mrs Vavasour occupied a house standing at the point where King's Square and Colliergate now meet; its archway crossed the entrance to St Andrewgate.

On 2 August 1577, Margaret and her husband appeared before the High Commission for Clauses Ecclesiastical (Province of York). This possibly sat in that part of the North Transept of York Minster where the Consistory Court was held; the Commissioners present included Archbishop Sandys, Dean Hutton, and the Chancellor, William Palmer. For her obstinate recusancy, Margaret Clitherow was imprisoned in York Castle, where she remained until the following February (Figure 4). She was sent there again in October 1580, being released for childbirth in April 1589.

The prisoners were housed in this period, not in Clifford's Tower but in a more modern building within the castle enclosure, near to the great stone entrance that faced Fishergate.

After her first release from prison, Margaret persuaded one of her near adjoining neighbours, both of whom were relatives of her husband and were recusants themselves for a short time, to let her prepare a secret room in their house where a visiting priest might be sheltered in safety and where Mass might be said. After Mrs Vavasour's house was raided in August 1581, the house in the Shambles became the principal centre for the celebration of the Catholic Mass in York.

Between the years 1582 and 1583 five priests, almost all of whom had been Margaret's spiritual directors, were arrested, tried and condemned at York on charges of high treason and executed on the Knavesmire. For a brief period Margaret, together with a few like-

Figure 4. A nineteenth century engraving of the entrance to York Castle.

Figure 5. The old Ouse Bridge.

minded women, found it possible to make what she described as her 'pilgrimage' to the site of their martyrdom. Under cover of darkness they passed down the Shambles, through Pavement, High and Low Ousegate to the old Ouse Bridge (Figure 5) then hump-backed and narrow with five arches carrying houses and shops, which was all demolished between 1809 and 1820, when the present, wider bridge was built. Up Micklegate to the Bar they went, and out along Blossom Street and the road now called The Mount (known then as St James' Hill) to the gallows site, today marked with a commemorative stone. Here Margaret 'earnestly wished (if it were God's will) for the same Catholic cause to end her life', and here 'she hoped one day God should be glorified in the memory of His martyrs'. 'As I remember', says her contemporary biographer, Father John Mush, 'she went barefoot to the place, and kneeling on her bare knees even under the gallows, meditated and prayed so long as her company would suffer her'.

On 8 March 1583 Margaret was committed to the Castle for the third time, after a trial at the Quarter Sessions, where the Justices of the Peace were now empowered to deal with recusancy cases. There was a large number of such cases, but a special jury was summoned to deal with Margaret Clitherow and an apothecary named John Wright, who was also sent to York Castle. The court probably sat in the

Guildhall, where Margaret was to appear again on a later occasion.

She was released during the year 1584 and placed under house arrest. Father Mush describes how she spent her day in that house, beginning with an hour an a half or two hours kneeling in prayer in her own room, 'meditating upon the Passion of Christ, the benefits of God bestowed upon her' and upon her own sins. Usually one or other of the hunted priests was secretly lodged in the room to which she had access, so that most mornings Margaret was able to hear Mass. 'If God's priests dare venture themselves to my house, I will never refuse them', she declared.

Sometimes Margaret was able to gather ten or twelve poor Catholics into her house for Mass and the sacraments, providing them also with a meal, served by herself, and assisting them with money from her ample allowance. She was, however, in charge of her husband's shop, and from the moment she opened its shutters and hung out the joints she was fully occupied with trade. At four o'clock she would retire to her room and pray for an hour with her children, whom she also instructed, and she ended the day with another hour of prayer and examination of conscience.

Besides the itinerant priests, there was now another man hidden in the house, Brian Stapleton, who had escaped after several years of imprisonment in the Castle. He was employed to teach Margaret's children secretly in a room in the attic.

During the afternoon of 10 March 1586 the Sheriffs of York raided the house of Margaret Clitherow. The priest and his companions immediately escaped by a secret route, followed by the schoolmaster, Brian Stapleton, but not before the latter had been seen by the

Figure 6. A nineteenth century engraving showing the entrance to the King's Manor.

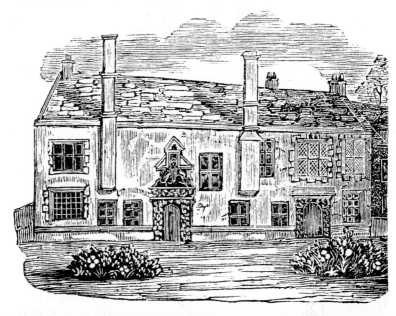

searchers. Thereupon Margaret, the children and the servants were carried off to King's Manor, then the headquarters of the Queen's Council in the north (Figure 6). Their route took them through King's Square and along Low and High Petergate, and through Bootham Bar, before turning to the left and entering the former precincts of St Mary's Abbey.

In the Manor House (formerly the residence of the Abbot of St Mary, but in part reconstructed and extended by the third Earl of Huntingdon, Lord President of the Council, as early as 1578, and further altered in modern times) Margaret was closely questioned, accused and threatened, but made light of her danger. At the same time, however, a foreign boy who shared her children's lessons was bullied into revealing the whereabouts of the secret room in the Shambles property, and here great quantities of vestments and plate and other requirements for performing Mass were found, besides signs of recent occupation.

At about seven o'clock Margaret was transferred once more to York Castle. The simplest way to take her there avoiding a repetition of the jostling through the narrow, over-populated streets, would have been by boat from the old abbey landing at the end of Marygate. It is known that Margaret arrived at the Castle soaked to the skin although there had been no rain, 'glad to borrow all kinds of apparel to shift her with'. She offered no explanation and made no complaint of her condition, but five years earlier a ducking-stool had been set up in St George's Close, by the river and near the Castle, so perhaps the sheriff's sergeants had made sport with her by ducking Margaret in the river.

On Monday, 14 March 1586, the first day of the Assizes, immediately after dinner, Margaret was brought from York Castle to the Guildhall to hear her indictment read (Figure 7). She was probably taken by river again to the landing-stage at the entrance to Common Hall Lane, an ancient tunnel aligned with Stonegate, one of the main streets of York in Roman times. At the Guildhall, then more usually called Common Hall, the Assizes for the city were held, the criminal cases being heard at the far, west end.[1] On this site Margaret, alone and without counsel, heard the charge against her - that she had feloniously harboured Father Francis Ingleby.[2] The penalty for harbouring a priest was death by hanging, and this Margaret fully expected, though she strongly denied knowing or maintaining any persons who were not the Queen's friends. However, the legal position was altered by her steadfast refusal to be tried by a jury picked by the very sheriff who had searched her house. The judge warned Margaret that persistence may result in a 'sharp death' reserved by the law for those who adopted this attitude, and gave her a night's respite to reconsider.

Margaret was not taken back to York Castle, but to the New Counter, known as John Trewe's House, a superior prison forming part of the huddle of corporation buildings on the north-west side of Ouse Bridge. She was taken along Coney Street, past her old parish church, and then past the church of St Michael, in Spurriergate, and so down Low Ousegate and over the bridge to the former chantry chapel dedicated to St William of York.[3] The upper portion of the chapel, converted into a dwelling house by the addition of flooring, made a continuation of the prison, which adjoined the small Council Chamber and the two Kidcote Prisons.

Here Margaret Clitherow spent the last ten days of her life. She was returned to the Guildhall on 15 March but continued her refusal to utter the formal words that would initiate her trial. Her reasons, she told a friend later, were to prevent her children and servants from giving evidence against her, and to spare the jury, many of whom she knew personally, from the sin of finding her guilty to please the Council in the North. A third reason may have been to protect her neighbours, who in the house of one, the priest was now secretly lodged, according to Father Mush. One of these neighbours was John Clitherow's sister; the other was a relative of his first wife.

In the absence of any cooperation from Margaret, the judge eventually had reluctantly to pronounce the terrible medieval penalty known as *peine forte et dure* upon her, and she was taken back to the New Counter by the sergeants carrying halberds and with her arms pinioned to prevent her still 'dealing money on both sides as she could' to the poor. 'Some of the Bench', we are told, 'sent to mark her countenance as she was carried forth of the Hall... all were astonished to see her of so good cheer.'

Figure 7. The Guildhall across the river Ouse showing the watergate entrance. *Alan Whitworth*

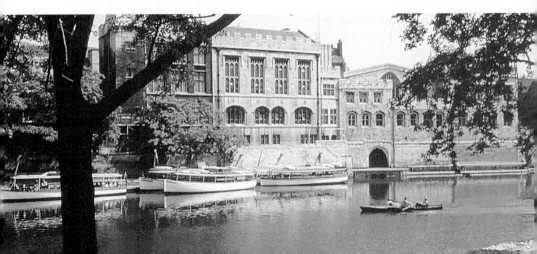

Figure 8. A Catholic martyr being crushed to death beneath weights.

At eight o'clock on the morning of Friday, 25 March 1586, the two sheriffs of York came to the New Counter, where Margaret was 'ready expecting them', and took her across the road, still emptying her purse to the throngs of poor, for the street 'was so full of people that she could scarce pass by them'.

Asked to pray for Queen Elizabeth I, she did so, but first she prayed 'for the Catholic Church, then for the Pope's Holiness, Cardinals, and other Fathers that have charge of souls, and then for all Christian Princes...' and especially for Elizabeth, Queen of England, that God turn her to the Catholic faith, and that after this mortal life she may receive the blessed joys of heaven. For I wish as much good to her Majesty's soul as to mine own'.

The sentence was to be carried out in the Tollbooth, directly opposite the prison. This was the office of the Collector of Bridge Tolls, which later formed part of another group of corporation buildings (all swept away by 1820). Margaret was taken inside, stripped naked and laid on the cold stone floor with a sharp stone placed under her back. Her arms were then bound to two posts by strings, and upon her was then put a heavy wooden door (Figure 8). At this point great weights were laid upon Margaret 'which when she first felt, she cried, "Jesu! Jesu! Jesu! Have mercy on me!" These were

Figure 9. The Shambles as it is today. *Alan Whitworth*

the last words she was heard to speak. She was in dying one quarter of an hour'.

Margaret Clitherow was beatified in 1929, and canonised together with thirty-nine other English and Welsh martyrs by Pope Paul VI on 25 October 1970. Today, a house in the Shambles is a shrine to her memory, visited by numerous pilgrims, a quiet place of contemplation in a street of great busyness (Figure 9).

Notes and References

1. The present Guildhall is a replica of that destroyed by German bombs in April 1942, when only the walls were left standing.
2. Son of Sir William Ingleby, who rebuilt Ripley Castle. Francis was later arrested, condemned for his priesthood and executed on the Knavesmire on 3 June 1586.
3. It is said that at that spot when a previous bridge collapsed in 1154, prayers to St William of York had ensured that no lives were lost.

8. The Early Coaching Days and Inns of York

by Alan Whitworth

COACHING IN ITS INFANCY was not just about travel, it was about a way of life (Figure 1). A person did not just board at the beginning of the journey and sit quietly to its conclusion. For a start,

Figure 1. Setting out by stagecoach from York through Micklegate Bar.

roads were often rough, and progress was slow. It was not unknown for passengers to have to get out and walk a distance over a particularly bad stretch. This made for intercourse between fellow travellers and, of course, the driver. And the time a journey took too, possibly meant an overnight stop. Accommodation could often be a hit and miss affair. Yet despite the hazards and difficulties, people travelled in large numbers from the commencement of the coaching era in the mid-seventeenth century to its demise towards the end of the nineteenth, hardly giving a thought to the problems of time and distance.

Extracts from personal diaries and letters often graphically illustrate the state of the highways, the dangers of coach travel, and the romance of the road. As early as 1678 there was a coach running between York and Hull in the summertime. This same coach is mentioned by Ralph Thoresby, the historian, in his diary, on his arrival from Holland at Hull, where his father met him in a hired coach as the stagecoach had finished for the season:

> *November 1678. From Hull we came by coach to York, and thence on horseback to Leeds. The stage coach being over for the winter... . It*

*proved a mortification to us both that he was as little able to endure
the effeminacy of this way of travelling as I was to ride on horseback.*

In 1683 there was a London coach running from York, through
Tadcaster, Ferrybridge, and Doncaster; and Leeds passengers were
obliged to ride on horseback to either York or Ferrybridge to join the
coach. After this coach was established it continued to run regularly,
and is the same vehicle mentioned in the coaching bill given
elsewhere (page 89).

Thorseby described his journey to London and back by this coach
at some length writing:

*February 19 1683. Up pretty timely preparing for a journey, and
somewhat concerned about the company, and fearful of being confined
to the coach for so many days with unsuitable persons.*

They stayed at Doncaster the first night, Newark the second,
Stamford the third, Bugden the fourth, Stevenage the fifth arriving at
London on the sixth day. We find him returning on the 4 April in the
same year, the return journey occupying only four days, the difference
being due probably to better weather as the year advanced, and
therefore better road conditions and an improved rate of travelling.

The year 1662 saw the first Act of Parliament passed for making
turnpike roads. From that date a slight improvement may be said to
have occurred, as very shortly afterwards there were additional
coaches running between London, York, Chester, and Exeter, each
having forty horses on the road. Still the highways remained very
bad, as ratepayers strongly opposed the *Turnpike Act*. According to
the diary of Sir Walter Calverley, of Leeds, in 1694, it took about four
days to travel from Doncaster to London. The state of perfection to
which coaching was brought, when in the height of its glory, will be
seen from the fact that in 1815 the Leeds Union did the distance
between London and Doncaster (162 miles) in sixteen and a half
hours, which included two hours for stoppages. However, there was
little improvement made in the rate of travelling up to the year 1706,
as will be observed from the following copy of an old coach bill
advertising a new service, which was preserved at the *Black Swan*, in
York for some years:

YORK Four Days
Stage-Coach.
Begins on Friday *the* 12th of April 1706.
ALL that are desirous to pass from London to York,

or from *York* to *London,* or any other Place
on that Road; Let them Repair to the *Black Swan* in
Holbourn in London, and to the *Black Swan* in *Coney
Street in York.*
At both which Places, they may be received in a
Stage Coach every *Monday, Wednesday* and *Friday,*
Which performs the whole Journey in Four Days, (*if
God permits*). And lets forth at Five in the Morning.
And returns from *York* to *Stamford* in two days,
and from *Stamford* by *Huntingdon* to *London* in two
days more. And the like Stages on their return.

There is no mention of any Leeds coach running in connection with
either of the above London coaches until 1708, when a coach
appears to have been started between Leeds and London or Leeds
and York in connection with the London coach. Thoresby says this
was so popular that all the places were sometimes booked a fortnight
in advance. A few years later there seems to have been another coach
started from Leeds in connection with the Wakefield coach, and
touching these coaches is the following entry in Thoresby's diary:

*May 17, 1708 - Preparing for a journey to York. Lord, grant thy
favourable presence from sin and all dangers. We found the way very
deep, and in some places dangerous for a coach (that we walked on
foot), but the Lord preserved us from all evil accident, that we got to
our journey's end in safety, blessed be to God.*

On the return journey to York, Thoresby tells us that he had to rise
between three and four in the morning in order to catch the coach,
which was hastened on its way by a Captain Crome, who happened
to be travelling by the same coach on the Queen's business, so that
they, 'got to Leeds by noon, blessed be God for mercies to me and
my poor family.' So dangerous was coach travel considered, even by
those establishing and running routes, that many coaching bills
suggested that those boarding made out their last will and testament!

In 1754 there was introduced a coach with springs, which was
described as a two-end glass coach machine, exceedingly light and
easy, to go from Edinburgh to London in ten days in summer and
twelve in winter. And now the roads started to improve and the speed
of coaches began to be greatly accelerated. In 1768 a new coach
called 'The Fly' began running between Leeds and London, and
actually performed the entire journey in two and a half days; and a
year later there was yet another coach started, doing the same

distance in the same time. By the year 1775 there were no less than four hundred coaches on the highways in different parts of the country.

On 24 July 1785, the first Royal Mail coach ran from London to Yorkshire, through Sheffield, Barnsley, and Wakefield, to Leeds (Figure 2). On the 16 October the following year, the first Mailcoach from London, by the Great North Road, set forth on its journey (Figure 3). From the last quarter of the eighteenth century to the beginning of the nineteenth, coaching made rapid strides. When at its height, in about 1835, there were no less than seven hundred Mail coaches running in Great Britain and Ireland, while the number of stagecoaches had increased by the same proportion. By a superior and more durable system of road-making, brought into vogue by McAdam, the speed of the Mails was greatly increased, the best coaches doing their regular average of ten miles an hour. Indeed, in 1836, the London and Edinburgh Mail did the whole distance of four hundred miles in forty five and a half hours, which included all stoppages. These being deducted left the average time at close on ten miles an hour and this coach did the 197 miles from York to London in twenty hours, which time included stoppages for changing horses.

Of the four principal inns in York connected with the road they each had their separate and particular features. The Mails started from the *York Tavern*, which adjoined the post office, and the stage and light coaches from the *Black Swan*. The *George Inn* confined itself principally to the posting business, and *Etteridge's* provided relays of horses for nobility and gentry travelling in their own private carriages. Of these four houses the *York Tavern* was the most important (Figure 4).

Figure 2. A Mailcoach passing through a village in the early hours picks up mail bags from the post office without stopping.

Figure 3. The York Mail (built 1820s) preserved in the Science Museum, London, is one of the few surviving vehicles of its type.

When the Mails first began to run, the *York Tavern,* situated in St Helen's Square, was kept by a Mr Pulleyn, who was followed by a Mr Simpson as landlord, who kept the establishment up to the end of the coaching days. Mr Simpson, however, had nothing to do with horsing the Mails and post-coaches or in providing post-horses of any description beyond keeping a few to run a cab or two for the use of his customers or commercial gentlemen. The posting business was in the management of Messrs Cattle & Maddocks, who had control of the stables connected with the tavern, and they would stand from 130 to 150 horses on their extensive premises. The entrance to the stables was through a wide archway at the opposite corner of the inn to the church. Up this yard were the coach offices, while the post office was only a few yards away on the low side of St Helen's Square, which was very convenient for the Mails when changing horses.

Figure 4. The *York Tavern,* in St Helen's Square.

'Dobbin' Cattle, as he was called, was a silversmith before he began to purchase equines and entered upon the business of providing horses for the Mails in conjunction with Mr Maddocks, who came from Heslington, near York. These two likewise worked some of the coaches along with a Mr Barber, of the *Black Swan* stables. They also kept a few post-chaises and some five or six post-boys; but the *George Inn,* on the opposite side of Coney Street to the *Black Swan,* was the inn that had the monopoly of the posting.

Mr Cattle hailed from Sheriff Hutton, and when the coaches went off the road he retired to Groves House, where he spent the remainder of his days. When Mr Simpson left the *York Tavern* he was succeeded by a Mr Harker, who changed the name of the establishment to *Harker's Hotel.* Harker had been at one time butler to Colonel Croft, and in the latter part of the old coaching days had kept the *White Swan,* at York. During that period he horsed one of the Hull coaches, which nevertheless did not run from his own inn, but from the *York Tavern* and the *Black Swan.*

Mr Harker was a great lover of horseflesh and breeder of blood-stock, and he kept a breeding establishment and stud farm at Stillington. He bred principally for the market, although he had a few horses in training at Malton. However, the bulk of his yearlings were usually offered for sale at each successive race meeting.

The *Black Swan,* in Coney Street, York, worked so much in conjunction with the *York Tavern,* so far as stabling horses and running coaches, as to encourage the idea that the two establishments were joined instead of separate inns. Although the *Black Swan* is the older of the two, it cannot be considered as the oldest of the cities' coaching inns, though it was very probable that it was the first inn to which regular coaches began to run.

In 1706, there would probably not be more than half a dozen coaches on the road in the whole of Yorkshire, so that the *Black Swan* may safely be classed among the very earliest of the coaching inns. In 1701 the landlord was a Mr Harding, and when the Mails first began to run in 1786, it was kept by Mr F. Wrigglesworth. He horsed some of the old coaches, or diligences as they were then called, in conjunction with other proprietors; but shortly after this time Mr Wrigglesworth left the house for the *George Inn* on the opposite side of Coney Street. Wrigglesworth was succeeded at the *Black Swan* by a Mr Batty, who in turn was followed by Mr Clarke, and the establishment was at that period known as *Clarke's Hotel.* Mr Clarke died there, and his widow carried on the business until she married Mr James Barber, who had the longest and most extensive association with the inn, and was the best known of its occupants in connection with its coaching history. Interestingly, before he married Clarke's widow and took up inn keeping, like his contemporary and part coadjutor, Barber was a silversmith in premises close to the *Black Swan*.

Mr Barber and Messrs Cattle and Maddocks, mentioned previously, worked a great deal together, and almost had a monopoly of the coach and mail business in the city. This was of so extensive a nature that after a time Mr Barber gave up the management of the inn to a Mr Judd, and took up residence as a gentleman at Tang Hall, near York. However, he retained the long rows of stables that bordered each side of the yard, and still continued to horse the coaches. Mr Barber stood about 130 horses at the *Black Swan*, and the following (right) is a list of some of the coaches that took their daily departure from this inn and the *York Tavern* during their joint tenancies.

:ON. 127

The c... the George Inn Coach Office, are as follow :—

To London, the Wellington, at a quarter past four in the afternoon, and arrives in London next afternoon at half past three o'clock.
To Newcastle and Edinbro', the Wellington, at a quarter past two in the afternoon, and arrives at Newcastle the same night, and Edinbro' next night at eight o'clock.
To Selby and Leeds, at half past three o'clock in the afternoon.
To Scarbro' and Sheffield, (during the season), at two o'clock in the afternoon.

The "*Old Judges' Lodgings*," mentioned at page 106, were formerly opposite to this Inn.

THE BLACK SWAN INN, AND
COACH OFFICE,

Are a little beyond the Old Judges' Lodgings, the former being kept by Mr. Judd, and allowed to be by far the largest and the best Inn in the city.

The Coach Office is, and has long been, under the direction of Mr. Dobson, who has favoured the writer with the following official report of the times of arrival and departure of the different mails and post coaches which come to and go from that office :—

ARRIVALS.

	H.	M.			H.	M.	
Leeds Wellington	10	0	night.	Whitby Neptune	12	30	noon.
London Mail	5	0	evening.	Hull Trafalgar	1	0	afternoon.
Scarbro' Mail	8	0	evening.	Newcastle Wellington	3	45	afternoon.
Hull Mail	8	0	evening.	Leeds Blue	12	0	noon.
Manchester Mail	5	0	evening.	London Wellington	1	30	afternoon.
Carlisle Express	7	0	morning.	Edinbro' Mail	6	30	morning.
Newcastle Express	10	0	night.	Hull Mail	3	30	afternoon.
London Express	7	30	morning.	Manchester Mail	5	0	morning.
Leeds Highflyer	6	0	evening.	Scarbro' Blue	12	0	noon.
Sheffield Transit	1	30	afternoon.	Harrogate Tally-Ho	10	0	morning.

DEPARTURES.

	H.	M.	
Leeds, Manchester, Nottingham, and Kendal Wellington (Sundays excepted)	6	0	morning.
London Mail	7	0	morning.
Scarbro' Mail	7	0	morning.
Hull Mail	7	0	morning.
Leeds and Manchester Mail	7	0	morning.
Carlisle and Glasgow Express, every Monday, Wednesday, and Friday	8	0	morning.
Newcastle and Edinbro' Express (Sundays excepted)	8	0	morning.
London Express (Saturdays excepted)	11	0	morning.
Leeds and Manchester Highflyer, by Wetherby (Sundays excepted)	9	0	morning.
Sheffield and Birmingham Transit (Sundays excepted)	2	0	afternoon.
Whitby Neptune (Sundays excepted)	2	0	afternoon.
Hull Trafalgar (Sundays excepted)	2	0	afternoon.
Newcastle and Edinbro' Wellington	2	0	afternoon.
Leeds Blue (Sundays excepted)	2	0	afternoon.
London Wellington	4	0	afternoon.
Newcastle and Edinbro' Mail	5	0	evening.
Hull Mail	7	30	evening.
Manchester Mail	9	0	evening.
SUMMER COACHES.			
Scarbro' Old True Blue (Sundays excepted)	1	0	noon.
Harrogate Tally Ho (Sundays excepted)	2	0	afternoon.

Figure 5. A list of coach arrivals and departures from the *Black Swan* inn.

This lengthy list of coaches would, of course, be considerably augmented by the arrival of duplicate coaches. So that in the Scarborough and Harrogate 'Seasons' the daily arrivals and departures from these two inns, the *Black Swan* and the *York Tavern*, would be something in the region of sixty in number, which would undoubtedly test the resources of the vast stabling situated between the two establishments.

The *George Inn*, Coney Street, once occupied the site of Messrs Leake and Thorpe. It was a very old building, and had a most curious porch-way that was embellished with several fine carved bosses. This always held the position of being the principal posting-house in the city, and as early as the year 1700 we find that a man named Jubb had the stabling, and kept post-horses there, although at that early date there would be no coaches running from the inn.

Towards the end of the nineteenth century, the property was held by a Mrs Winn, who kept eight or ten post-boys, the foremost of whom were George Gill and a youth named Tiplady, and had a monopoly of almost all the posting-houses between York and Scarborough. At the end of the coaching era Mr Abraham Braithwaite kept the *George Inn*, but he later removed to the *Black Swan*. A coach called the 'Highflyer' used to operate daily from there to the *Blacksmith's Arms*, at Scarborough, and at another period a second Scarborough coach was horsed from the *George Inn* by Tom Poole, who afterwards moved to the *Greyhound*.

Etteridge's Hotel in Lendal was devoted entirely to the supply of horses for noblemen and gentlemen travelling post or in their own private carriages. The proprietor Mr Etteridge stood about forty horses at his own stables behind the inn. It was said that he lived there all his life, and ended his days there long after the coaching and posting days were dead. 'Tommy' Etteridge was a noted figure around York, and he was considered a character in his day. A gentleman of the old school, courteous in manner, and precise and methodical in all he did, he gained the thorough respect of all his fellow-citizens. It was his habit at some point to make a daily round of the city in his high gig, which he completely filled, for he is said to have weighed nigh upon twenty-four stones. Each morning saw him regularly pass through the Shambles and along the Market Place, exchanging the courtesies of the day with the tradesmen and others. Each successive evening would see him wending his way to the *Punch Bowl*, where he and a few other kindred spirits nightly assembled to discuss the daily budget of news gathered from the numerous coach guards and other sources. This latter custom he kept up to the end of his time, although in his later years he was obliged to call in the assistance of his groom. However he did not abandon his old habits, and leaning on the arm of his servant 'Tommy' Etteridge still made nightly pilgrimages to meet his old cronies.

Passing on to the smaller coaching inns of York we come to the *White Horse* in Coppergate. This was one of the oldest inns in the city, and was in existence long before public coaches began to run. Well before the Mails operated the house was kept by a Mrs Roscoe, and at the time the 'York and Leeds Diligence', which was horsed by Mr Wrigglesworth, ran from there to Mr Vincent's, at the *Golden Lion*,

Leeds. The fare was six shillings. In 1802 Mrs Elizabeth Roscoe sold the *White Horse* to her niece, Mary Coates, who had long assisted her in the business. Later, this house was kept by Mrs Mary Sowerby, who horsed the 'Royal Union Sheffield Coach' (removed from the *Swan and Tavern*) on the Tadcaster stage. This coach also ran to Scarborough at two in the afternoon, and Mr Charles Palmer, who had his coach office in the *White Horse* yard, where he stood his horses, operated it in conjunction with Mr Braithwaite, on the first stage to Scarborough.

The 'Harrogate Integrity' and the 'Pledge', running between York and Newcastle, were also worked from the *White Horse*.

The *White Swan*, Pavement, was kept in the latter part of the old coaching days by a Mr Woodhead. In the early part of the nineteenth century it was run by a Mrs Hardcastle, who retired from this coaching inn to *Calm Cottage*, on the Malton Road, where in due time she passed away. One of the coaches that ran from here in Mrs Hardcastle's tenancy was the 'York and Sheffield Accommodation', every afternoon at half past one, that went to the *King's Head*, at Sheffield. This coach was horsed by Mr Robinson on the Tadcaster stage, who stood his horses at the *White Swan*, and at one time stabled the Sheffield baggage wagons.

A light post-coach left the *White Swan* and the *Commercial Hotel*, at the corner of Nessgate, at half past eight each morning for Manchester, journeying by way of Tadcaster, Leeds, Huddersfield, and Oldham in ten hours. This coach also ran on to Liverpool, and was the only light post-coach that did the journey between York and Liverpool in a single day. It was driven by Isaac Robson, who likewise horsed the coach, and stood his horses at the *White Swan*.

The 'Royal Union' was a Leeds and Scarborough coach, that left the *White Swan* daily for both places.

There was a second 'Royal Union' post-coach which ran from this establishment in Mr Woodhead's time to Mr Lewis's, *Humber Tavern*, in Hull.

Mr Woodhead never horsed any of the coaches from the *White Swan*. This business was in the hands of a Mr Robinson, to whom he let the stables. When Mr Woodhead came to the inn he considerably enlarged it. He was the possessor of a famous bay mare, a celebrated trotter, which regularly attended the Doncaster races along with its owner. When the St Leger winner passed the post the bay mare was put on her mettle, and for many years they were the first to bring the news to York, where they were anxiously awaited by crowds of sporting Yorkshiremen. Mr Woodhead was a native of Hull. He died very suddenly while entertaining a large party of guests at a ball at his own home.

The *Elephant and Castle Inn*, Skeldergate, was kept early in the nineteenth century by Mr George Flower, who was succeeded by a Mr Taylor. The following coaches ran from this house: the Yorkshire Hussar (York and Ripon), the Harrogate Union, the Recovery (Leeds and Scarborough), the Wensleydale Umpire, and the Hull Union before it was transferred to the *White Swan*.

The *Old Sand Hill Inn*, in Colliergate, long since demolished, and which once occupied the site of the Volunteer Drill Shed, was kept by a Mrs Monkman. She, in conjunction with Isaac Robson, horsed the Leeds and Scarborough coaches and the Royal Umpires. From this inn also ran a pair-horse dilligence, driven by Tommy Raper, every Tuesday, Thursday, and Saturday, for Malton and Scarborough.

The *Commercial Inn and Coffee House* which stood at the corner of Nessgate, later renamed the *Coach and Horses*, was at one time kept by a Tom Waites, who committed suicide in his bedroom. The house was then taken over by James Douglas, who was acknowledged to be one of the best drivers on the road. It was said that he was a quiet, retiring little man, rather inclined to stoutness, with round, contented features. He was very abstemious and would never go beyond the single glass he allotted himself. His style of driving was the very opposite of another celebrated coachman, Tom Holtby. In Waites' manner there was no display or ostentation, but it rather partook of skill and science of the quietest and most polished kind.

Figure 6. A Victorian stagecoach in the York Castle Museum.

The 'Royal Umpire' left here for Leeds every afternoon at four o'clock, and another 'Royal Umpire' left at the same time every Tuesday, Thursday, and Saturday in the opposite direction for Malton. These coaches were horsed by Isaac Robson and T. Raper, and were afterwards removed to the *White Swan*.

The *Robin Hood Inn*, Castlegate, was kept by Mr Clayton, but Mr William Flower horsed the coaches that worked from this establishment. These were the Providence, running from York to Selby each morning at seven in order to meet the Hull Steam Packet boat, after the arrival of which, it returned to York the same day. At a later period they operated the Steam Packet Company's own coach which ran to Selby, Hull, and Leeds every morning at six o'clock (Figure 6).

The *Pack Horse Inn*, Micklegate was run by a Mr Hornsey, but again, like so many other establishments, the horses were operated by another, in this instance, Mr Joseph Riccall, who kept the *Half Moon,* in Blake Street. The original 'Light Post' coach from York to Ripon, and the 'Highflyer', which left the *Black Swan,* in Middleham, at five in the morning and arrived there at noon every Monday, Wednesday, and Friday, returning the following days at two in the afternoon, were worked from the *Pack Horse Inn.*

As an aside, in recounting the deeds of the old coaching days, one should not forget those who made the many coach journeys possible. Those intrepid and often charismatic 'knights of the road', who in all weathers, and through often arduous conditions, endeavoured to get the passengers to their destination as safely and quickly as possible - the coachmen.

Of all the many who operated out of York city, possibly the most noted was Tom Holtby, the crack Yorkshire coachman. He lived there for a time, and had some property in Tower Street, where he died on 1 June 1863 aged seventy-two. Holtby was the pride of the country as a coachman; described as tall, gentlemanly-looking, of good presence, with a smart, showy style of driving and a dash of confident recklessness which commanded attention and admiration, and gained for him the nickname of 'Rash Tom'.

He was born in 1791 and began life as a post-boy at Easingwold with Benjamin Lacy, who kept the head inn at that place, the *Rose and Crown.* It was not, however, until he was twenty-nine years of age that Tom Holtby became a regular coachman, but he rapidly worked his way upwards until he became the recognised head of his profession. More than twenty years on the box seat were spent during the heyday of coaching. Then in the prime of life, he was privileged to enjoy its sweetest favours. Fortune was kind to him, and when the end came and coaching declined, it left him in anything but mean circumstances. He outlived the demise of the road by some twenty years, and his active restless spirit launched him into various speculations, many of which sadly turned out to be more, or less failures.

When the coaches went off the road he first took to horse-breaking, among other things, for the neighbouring gentry, but more as a hobby than from necessity. By teaching young gentlemen the intricacies of his art, and from the numerous other lucrative sources that the road offered, this 'Prince' of coachmen acquired a pretty considerable competence. Yet at one period, moving to Haxby a few miles out of York, Holtby purchased an extensive brickyard; but there was no affinity between coaching and brick making, and the venture did not prosper. He also became part owner of a newspaper and dropped £600 by the move, as he did another £800 when the Agricultural Bank took a tumble, and various sums by other banks. Nevertheless, with all this hard luck, he died worth £3,000 so that he must have been a rich man in his best days. Tom Holtby was a constant attendant at York Races, and had a few racehorses in training with John Scott at Malton, but towards the end of his life the handsome figure often noted in the ring, sadly began to break up. On his death, he was buried in the churchyard at Haxby, where a simple upright stone marks his grave.

Holtby at one time drove the 'Highflyer', but the 'Edinburgh Mail' was the coach with which he had the longest association. This celebrated Mail was put on the road on the 16 October 1786, and ran from the *Bull and Mouth,* London, by way of Ware, Royston, Huntingdon, Stilton, Stamford, Newark, East Retford, Bawtry, Doncaster, Ferrybridge, Tadcaster, York, Thirsk, Northallerton, Darlington, Durham, Newcastle, Morpeth, Alnwick, Berwick, Dunbar, Musselburgh, and Leith, to Edinburgh. This coach continued along the given way for a great number of years, although there were various changes of route during its time. During one period it ran through Stevenage, and towards the end of its days it operated from Doncaster to York by way of Askern and Selby, instead of by Ferrybridge and Tadcaster. This new line of road was shorter by about three miles, and as time on these fast coaches was always an object of consideration, no opportunity was lost in diminishing the rate of travelling.

The time allowed from London to Edinburgh in the best days of the Mail was forty-two hours twenty-three minutes, and the time from London to York (197 miles) was twenty hours fifty-four minutes. These times included all stoppages for changes of horse, and the average rate of travelling was about nine and a half miles per hour!

The Edinburgh Mail was worked by three companies, the first owned the ground between London and York, the second that between York and Newcastle, and the third ran forward to Edinburgh. The Mail continued to operate without intermission from 1786 until 1842, when it finally ceased (Figure 7). On the day of its last journey, it was running over the new line of road from Doncaster, via Selby. The road at that time passed by and for some distance lay contiguous to Escrick Park, the seat of Lord Wenlock, who was an amateur coachman of no mean order. His lordship sent his footman to the park gates to ask Tom Holtby if he would drive through the park and out at the other gates. In the park Lord Wenlock, with a team of four horses in his private drag, and Sir John Lister Kaye with a similar team, met the Mail in order to be in at the death of this famous coach. They then accompanied it with all due ceremony as guard of honour on its final run to the ancient city of York.

They hoisted a huge black flag from the coach roof and Lord Wenlock took the ribbons, with Holtby sitting beside him on the box-seat, and in this style they entered York and drew up in front of the *Black Swan* for the last time.

'Remember the coachman, sir,' said the baronet, slyly touching his hat and nudging Tom with his elbow. 'So I will,' answered Tom, 'if your lordship will likewise remember the guard.' 'Well, I'll give him double what you give me.'

'Done,' replied Holtby, as he whipped a five pound note into Lord Wenlock's hand. It was with a somewhat rueful face that his lordship handed ten pounds to the guard, Tom Day; but he remarked as he did so: 'I have had you for five pound, anyhow, Tom.' 'Not a bit of it,

Figure 7. The mud-spattered York Mail changing horses outside a hostelry. At such times passengers might take the opportunity to have a drink.

Figure 8. The *Mail Coach Inn,* St Sampson's Square, now named the Roman Baths after a Roman bath was discovered inside.

Figure 9. The *Black Swan,* Peasholme Green, one of the oldest coaching inns in York.

my lord; Day and I understand each other; I shall clear £2 10s by the transaction.' And so it was by such incidents, tales and events that the romance of the coaching days was kept alive.

At the other end of some of the principal Mail routes, many set off from Leeds, in particular the *Rose and Crown*, in Briggate. The oldest established of these coaches was the old Manchester and Liverpool Mail. This coach began running in the year 1792, and was then and for a number of years afterwards known as the 'York and Liverpool Mail'. It ran from York by way of Tadcaster (from which place it was horsed by Mr John Hartley, the postmaster, and Mr William Backhouse) to Leeds, where it continued through Halifax, Rochdale, Manchester, Warrington, to the *Cross Keys*, Dale Street, Liverpool, taking at that time eighteen hours to complete the journey. In 1807 it ceased to run through York, but continued on the

Figure 10. An old ostler propping up the stable door. A large number of people, beside coachmen, depended for their livelihood on the coaching business.

old route from Leeds to Liverpool. In this year the 'York Highflyer' was put on the road, and the Liverpool Mail ran in connection with it, and thus it ran until 1838, with but little alteration save that of improved time. In this year, almost at the end of its days, it was removed from the house that had known it so long to the *Albion*, in Leeds, and started to run over a new line of road via Huddersfield, to end at Manchester only, and doing the thirty-nine miles in just under four hours. It remained at the *Albion* until it went out of service.

In 1821 the *York Morning Mail* commenced running from the *Rose and Crown*, leaving at four o'clock. In 1836 this coach was transferred to the *Golden Lion*.

Of the *Rose and Crown* coaches the next in importance to the Mails was the Highflyer, York, Leeds, Manchester, and Liverpool coach, which started running on 5 December 1807. Leaving the *York Tavern* at six each morning, and arriving at the *Rose and Crown*, it set out immediately for Bradford, Halifax, and Manchester, where it arrived

Figure 11. Major Tomlinson, a provincial coach proprietor who drove the coach.

at six in the evening and stayed all night. Next day it set out at seven o'clock in the morning for Liverpool, returning there at four each evening. Passengers slept at Manchester and left the following morning for Leeds and York. This coach was horsed from Leeds by a Mr Musgrave, and for a short time was worked from the *Bull and Mouth.* In time it again returned to its old quarters at the *Rose and Crown* and after running for a few years as above, it devolved into two separate concerns, although running in connection, which were afterwards respectively known as the 'York and Manchester Highflyers'.

The 'York Highflyer' left the *Rose and Crown* each afternoon at half past three, by way of Tadcaster, until 1829, when it ran over a new line of road through Roundhay, near Leeds, Collingham, Wetherby, Bickerton, Marston, Rufforth, and Acomb, to arrive at the *York Tavern.*

In the year 1807, shortly after Manchester and Liverpool Mail ceased to operate through to York, the Whitby and Scarborough Mail was begun. This left the *Rose and Crown* at six each evening, and ran by way of York and Malton, on Tuesdays, Thursdays, and Sundays, to Whitby and, on other days, to Scarborough. It ultimately became a daily service to York in connection with the York, Whitby and Scarborough Mails, and so continued to run to the end of the coaching era.

The end of the coaching era came about quite swiftly at the start of the transport revolution that saw the railways cover the country. Stiff competition from the 'iron horse' soon put paid to the long hauls, as the network of railways first began to shorten the routes between, firstly, principal towns and cities and later, all manner of villages and stops. Soon, with the increase in reliability and the speed of trains, the journey time from the capital to York, Edinburgh and such places was reduced to hours rather than days - and so the coach finally went off the road, passengers preferring the comfort and speed of this new form of 'coaching'.

9. 'Bombers Away!' The Story of RAF Elvington

by Ian Richardson

THINK OF YORK and immediately images of the layers of past civilisations upon which the present city stands spring to mind. The Roman walled city, fierce Vikings sailing up the rivers aboard their longboats, York Minster standing proudly as a testament to the Christian influence along with the other splendid architecture of medieval, Tudor, Georgian and Elizabethan times are all aspects of York's diverse past. Add to this York's long association with the confectionary and railway industries, the Sport of Kings and simply the beautiful scenery and it is plain to see why this rich tapestry of heritage makes the city such an ever popular tourist destination.

But there is more. There is in fact an aspect of York's history that is almost forgotten. Almost, but not quite! Thanks mainly to a dedicated group of volunteers and their followers a fading piece of history has been preserved. This forms the base from which the story of both York and Yorkshire's connection with one of the greatest achievements of mankind can be told.

I am of course talking about the wonder of flight, aviation, call it what you will. This is the triumph of man against the elements that so many of us take for granted as we jet off on our holidays to destinations around the globe. How many of us realise how, and where, it all began? However, let us move forward in time from the roots of aviation to a period when the power and potential of flight really came into its own. This is a period that is remembered proudly by some, quietly so by others and almost wilfully forgotten by others still who are scarred by painful memories. Many of the younger generations amongst us have little knowledge of the sacrifice that went before them. The time we are entering is the period between 1939 and 1945 when great nations came again into conflict through the actions of a few.

Soon after the outbreak of the Second World War it was realised that whoever had command of the air would almost certainly emerge as the victorious force. Consequently, it was not long before the skies over much of rural England were filled with the sight and sound of thousands of heavy bombers as they went off on their missions of destruction in response to the similar aggression hurled at our own cities, towns and homes.

By late 1940, the hunt was on in earnest to find suitable sites to build the bases from which these aircraft would operate. Yorkshire and Lincolnshire, with open spaces and high, flat terrain, were prime locations. The Air Ministry Aerodrome Board acquired just such a site at a location near the village of Elvington, only five miles south-east of the centre of York. In 1941, contractors moved in to build the Class A heavy bomber airfield, which had initially been planned as a grass airfield, but was actually built with three concrete runways. RAF Elvington was born, to become one of the most unique of all Bomber Command Stations in England (Figure 1). The base was completed in September 1942 and became part of No 4 Group, Bomber Command, whose headquarters had relocated to Heslington Hall, York, in April 1940. Has fate intervened to bring me to be writing this article just as the 60th anniversary of this event passes? Heslington Hall now forms part of the administrative campus of the University of York.

The 5 October 1942 saw the arrival of No 77 Squadron from their former base at Chivenor, where the squadron had been engaged in anti-submarine activities as part of Coastal Command, initially being equipped with the slow and ungainly, but nevertheless sturdy and reliable Armstrong Whitley aircraft. These were duly replaced with the four-engine Handley Page Halifax III (Figure 2). The early weeks of 77 Squadron's arrival were spent on conversion from one aircraft type to another before the inexorable bombing raids over the German industrial heartland commenced in earnest. This was the

Figure 1. Bomber crews at RAF Elvington air base during the Second World War.

Figure 2. The Handley Page Halifax Mk III bomber.

storm unleashed after the seemingly innocuous warnings given to the German nation by the leaflet raids that commenced immediately after war was declared in September 1939. In fact, earlier in that year, Goering had proclaimed to the German people that no bombs would ever fall on German soil, but the RAF were litter bombing on the second night of the war! Many of these raids were carried out by aircraft from No 4 Group based at other local airfields, including 77 Squadron based at the time at Driffield, before moving to Chivenor. Amazingly, many of these leaflets, or 'nickels' as they were known due to the fine protective nickel coating, survive and examples can be seen on display at the Yorkshire Air Museum.

The attrition rate suffered by Bomber Command was inevitably high, with the average loss rate being around 4 per cent from the typical squadron strength of 18 to 20 aircraft. Given that each Halifax carried a crew of seven, the cost in human terms was even greater. By the end of the war, 77 Squadron had lost some eighty Halifax aircraft, with those crewmen being killed, captured or listed as missing in action numbering over 500. In fact, the average life span of a bomber crew was just six weeks and only a mere two weeks for the most isolated and vulnerable of all crew members, the rear gunner, or 'tail end Charlie' as they were affectionately, but unflatteringly, known (Figure 3). These are sobering statistics for the young of today to reflect upon, as these brave young men were barely out of their teens when they were called to the defence of their country.

In 1944, an event took place to make RAF Elvington unique among all bomber command stations. Airmen of French nationality had been serving with squadrons around the country for some time, but in May 1944 it was realised that there were enough of them to form their own squadron. RAF Elvington was duly chosen to be their base. On the 15 May 1944, 77 Squadron left their home of two years for a new base at nearby Full Sutton and, on the next day, the Free

Figure 3. Crews of 77 Bomber Squadron, based at RAF Elvington among which is Mr Ralph Tailforth, one of the most devoted and long serving of the museum volunteers.

French Air Force moved in with the formation of No 346 'Guyenne' Squadron. This was followed shortly by No 347 'Tunnisie' Squadron, with both of these going on to play a major role in the bombing campaign in the latter stages of the war. There were some 2,000 French personnel stationed at the base, so it was little wonder that RAF Elvington, together with the village, became known locally as 'Little France'.

The French squadrons were in action on both day and night bombing raids right until the end of the war and, in fact, the last German aircraft to crash on British soil was a Junkers JU88 night fighter chasing a French crewed Halifax back to its base at Elvington. The JU88, flying perilously low, hit a tree and crashed into a farmhouse near to the airfield, killing the crew of four and two members of the household. This tragic occurrence took place in early

March 1945. A small memorial to loved ones lost can be seen outside the house on the road to Elvington village.

Following the end of hostilities, a frustrating period of inactivity ensued for the French personnel as they waited for the preparation of a new airfield in their homeland. On the 29 October 1945, the two squadrons finally flew out of RAF Elvington in their Halifaxes for the last time, with one of these tragically crashing shortly after take-off, killing three and seriously injuring eight others (Figure 4). On arrival in France, the squadrons effectively formed the base of the present French Air Force.

After the departure of the French, Elvington airfield came under the control of RAF Maintenance Command and was duly stripped of all equipment and stores. It remained in this virtually abandoned state until the advent of the Cold War. The East-West tensions had led the US Air Force to seek bases upon which to station their huge B52 strategic bombers and RAF Elvington was one of those bases given over for this purpose, among thirty others around the country. The United States government invested in the extension of the runway and pan and the construction of a new control tower. The 10,152 ft runway is one of the longest in Europe, with the concrete pan similarly at 49.374 acres being one of the largest military aprons ever built. In fact, the structure is one of the global landmarks that can be seen from space. The airfield was occupied by a small USAAF

Figure 4. The French squadrons' farewell parade, 20 October 1945.

Signals unit in 1954. The envisaged aircraft never materialised, however, due to a change in defence policy caused by the emergence of the Inter Continental Ballistic Missile as a long-range strategic defence weapon, making such aircraft as the B 52 virtually redundant.

In 1959, the base was handed back to the Royal Air Force and was designated as a V-Bomber dispersal point and the awesome Vulcan bombers could be seen on exercises in the early 1960s. From 1962 onwards, the airfield was used as a relief landing ground by pilots undergoing training at RAF Linton-on-Ouse and Church Fenton. Also during the 1960s, prototypes of the Blackburn Buccaneer, a fine Yorkshire military aircraft built at Brough, near Hull, were tested on the runway. The airfield served in this role for nearly thirty years until finally, on the 1 April 1992, even this activity ceased and RAF Elvington was closed.

Meanwhile, in the latter stages of the operational life of the airfield, new life was being breathed into the abandoned buildings of the wartime base, not used since those dark days of the Second World War. It was the French connection that was to be the key to the transformation of the former bomber command station into what is today a thriving and expanding Air Museum and Allied Forces Memorial. Many of the French personnel had married local people and visited Elvington regularly to attend an annual service at the French Memorial that had been erected in the village. This regular gathering was the signal to some dedicated local residents who were increasingly disturbed at the desolated state that the abandoned buildings were in. The realisation came that if the French veterans came regularly to see the memorial, then surely there must be many people who would come to see the preserved buildings where so many potent memories had been forged?

Accordingly, in 1983, a group of volunteers was formed, and,

Figure 5. The Memorial Garden dedicated to those members of the Allied Air Force who gave their lives during the 1939-45 campaign.

Figure 6. Constructed in 1942, the war-time control tower was the first area of the Yorkshire Air Museum to be restored.

under charitable status, began the long task of clearing away the years of decay and neglect. The Yorkshire Air Museum and Allied Forces Memorial rose from amongst the scene of dereliction (Figure 5). The first open day of the museum was held on the 11 August 1985, with the first opening to the general public coming on the 31 May 1986. Thanks also to the French, exhibits such as the control tower, which was the first building to be restored (Figure 6), and briefing room are authentically recreated, due to the discovery of a wartime archive film of the base in operation under French control. This film, depicting a bombing raid over Leipzig, is shown regularly at the museum and is a highly evocative piece of viewing for the visitors, who will recognise the display buildings they have just been admiring being used for their original purpose.

The land was at this time owned by the local firm William Birch and Sons Limited and the company offered the rent of the site at a generously nominal rate, subject to the drafting of a plan for development. This was duly done and the entirely self-supporting group worked hard to raise the capital to acquire the site from the ever supportive William Birch and Sons, with the purchase of the twelve-acre site being completed in 1993. The volunteer ethos is still very strong, with membership expanding greatly over the years, as more and more people discover the secret and wish to lend their support. There are now over 1,000 members, with some 250 of these being active in many roles around the site. Due to the RAF connections of some of the early volunteers, it was not long before word spread among the numerous Squadron Associations about the formation of the museum, with support coming in the establishment of displays and memorials and the holding of many annual reunions at the museum. The memorial aspect is at the forefront of the museums activities and the beautiful and peaceful Memorial Garden was planned from the beginning and is now maturing, providing a haven for relatives and visitors generally to sit and quietly reflect on the sacrifices made by so many.

Gradually, one building at a time was refurbished, with displays continuously moving around the site as more and more items of memorabilia were donated, a process which continues to this day. In fact, an archive of international importance has developed which contains examples of painstaking pieces of individual research into, for example, the records of all the Second World War RAF bases and the detailing of all aircraft crashes in Yorkshire during the war period. Some of these took decades to develop and the museum is the perfect home for such irreplaceable works. It is this slow, progressive development that sets the museum apart from many other exhibitions, particularly those that are nationally funded. These are usually created in one go and can never emulate the deep sense of personal involvement that can be experienced at Elvington. The Air Museum is however a non-profit making Charitable Trust, registered with the Museums and Galleries Commission and, as such, all artefacts acquired or donated become part of the national collection, preserved for the benefit of future generations.

Perhaps one of the most special features of the museum is the presence of many genuine veterans who actually served at RAF Elvington in both air and ground crew roles. An imposing stone memorial to 77 Squadron can be seen on entrance to the site and the history of the squadron can be traced in a dedicated display. The original 77 Squadron display was one of the first exhibits and has expanded over the years. Veterans such as these are joined by many others who flew many of the most illustrious aircraft of the war; Lancasters, Hurricanes, Spitfires, Mosquitoes, Liberators, the list goes on. The years may be catching up with these fine people, but the spirit that helped them survive horrific experiences can be seen in the time and dedication they give to building and maintaining exhibits and talking to visitors while they undertake various other duties. Perhaps the key to what brings so many visitors back again and again is the feeling that it really is a *living* museum where time however seems to have stood still.

In the fascinating and unique Air Gunners' Room (Figure 7), the grim reality of the gunners' existence can be appreciated as you see restored gun turrets, making one wonder how these men spent

Figure 7. The unique display of gun turrets in 'The Gunners Memorial Room', at the Yorkshire Air Museum. This collection is believed to be the only one of its type in the World.

sometimes over eight hours in such cramped and isolated positions. Brave men indeed. As you look at photographs of young men next to their aircraft, you may be approached by a sprightly 'young' 77-year-old, pointing to the image of himself aged just eighteen! The museum is 'home' to the National Air Gunners Association, 77 Squadron Association and 609 'West Riding' Fighter Squadron Association.

The museum is also known as the 'home of the Halifax', as the aircraft collection began in essence with the restoration project of the Handley Page HP59 Halifax MkIII LV 907. Work commenced in 1984, following the discovery of a 26ft long fuselage section being used as a chicken coop by a farmer on the Isle of Lewis in the Outer Hebrides! This section was flown to the museum underneath an RAF Chinook helicopter, with the transportation providing a highly valuable training exercise for the air force. Following the completion of the external restoration, the aircraft was officially 'rolled out' for public viewing on Friday 13 September 1996. To date, this aircraft is the only restored Halifax in the world. The aircraft has been decorated and named after the illustrious Halifax 'Friday the 13th', which flew 128 successful operations, including numerous day and night bombing raids. The 'unlucky' insignia on the aircraft may have worked in reverse and actually have been the aircraft's saving grace! Restoration is ongoing, with much of the interior now complete. The aircraft represents a magnificent tribute to all those who have spent many long hours on the project working often from old and somewhat faded drawings and documentation. Few visitors can fail to be stunned by its presence and the sight moves many surviving airmen to tears as they recall their connections with the aircraft. The Halifax was in fact known as the 'White Rose Bomber' as it predominantly flew from Yorkshire bases.

York's connection with the Halifax can also be traced to the former municipal airport at Clifton, which had come into existence after a long and frustrating period of indecision. Most of these civilian airfields were requisitioned during September 1939, with Clifton being used as a relief site for RAF Linton-on-Ouse. Whitley MKI aircraft of 'A' Flight, 51 Squadron were stationed on the airfield. Following the formation of No 4 Group's Headquarters at Heslington Hall, Clifton was used as the base for the Group's Communication Flight. In 1940, the grass strip was replaced with the 'traditional' three runway triangle favoured by Bomber Command. Although several squadrons flying various aircraft such as Lysanders, Austers and the American Curtiss Tomahawks and P51 Mustangs used the airfield during the course of the war, it was to be as a Civilian Repair Unit, under the control of Handley Page, that the airfield would be mainly associated. Accordingly, between the years of 1941 and 1948, hundreds of Haifaxes were both repaired and, sadly, scrapped here in their thousands, following decommissioning at the end of the war. No complete Halifax was ever kept for posterity, out of the 6,176 built, and it is indeed fitting that, through the Yorkshire Air Museum, York is now the place where the only restored example can be seen. It is worth noting that Norman Spence, museum member and magazine editor has written a fascinating account of the history of Clifton airfield, entitled *The Airport That Never Was*.

Another aspect of aviation in York that is almost forgotten but should not be overlooked is that of aircraft construction. After the tragic crash of the Howden built R101 airship, construction of these aircraft ceased with chief designer, Barnes Wallis, continuing his association with Vickers at another site. However, engineer and stress calculator Neville Shute Norway, along with A.H. Tiltman and Lord Grimethorpe formed an aircraft manufacturing company under the name of Airspeed Limited, with this company being based in the heart of York at premises in Piccadilly. In 1931, the company approached the corporation with a proposal to build a larger factory if a suitable airfield could be found. One of the long-standing objections of some corporation officials to the development of a proper airfield in York had historically been focused on the possible disruption to the sleep patterns of factory shift workers that aircraft flying would bring. As the wrangle for land continued, the AS-4 Ferry was produced, although not in significant numbers. The Corporation ultimately failed to find a suitable site, and Airspeed Limited moved to premises in Portsmouth following an attractive package of support. However, the design of the AS5 Courier by Neville Shute Norway was conducted in York and this was the first design to incorporate a retractable undercarriage. The superior aerodynamics that this provided was not at first appreciated by designers such as Sydney Camm (Hawker) and R.J. Mitchell (Supermarine) and was not included in the initial designs of either the Hurricane or Spitfire. However, production versions did have this feature, contributing to their improved performance.

Alas, it is not also widely known and appreciated that Yorkshire, at Brompton Dale near Scarborough, is actually the birthplace of manned flight in a 'conventional' fixed wing aircraft. Sir George Caley designed a glider type aircraft after separating the principles of lift and propulsion. In 1849, he proved that an un-powered glider with fixed wing could fly while supporting the weight of a child, aged about ten inside what resembled a small boat slung underneath the contraption. This was done on Brompton Dale in the summer of that year. Similarly, in 1852, an adult man, reputedly Caley's coachman, was flown in an improved design of this glider, incorporating a

Figure 8. Derek Piggott takes to the air at Brompton Dale in 1966 in a replica Cayley Glider, re-enacting the world famous event of 1852.

Figure 9. A lazy summer's day at RAF Elvington, July 1942 with an early Mark Halifax in the background and the ubiquitous NAAFI van in the foreground dispensing refreshments to ground crews.

rudder type system for controlling direction and height, from the same location. No drawings of these aircraft survive, but the design of the 1852 Caley Governable Parachute does and from this, in 1966, a replica was made for a TV Documentary, produced by Anglia Television. The replica was built with the objective of testing Caley's design. The incredible contraption was successfully flown, piloted, from Brompton Dale in the same manner as its predecessors all those years ago (Figure 8). Once again, it is fitting therefore, that the Yorkshire Air Museum has acquired this historic replica from the National Science Museum, where it is now on display to the public, close to its 'spiritual' home.

Indeed, today there is a rich vein of aviation and its accompanying social history to be discovered by both the tourist and resident alike at Elvington. From balloons in York in 1785, two years after the first manned balloon flight over Paris in 1783, to Caley and his gliders, through the Air Pageants of the early 1900s, to aircraft design and manufacture. The Yorkshire Air Museum provides the ideal location from which to base a journey of discovery into the wartime role of York and surrounding airfields and more.

So think of York and all those things mentioned at the beginning, but think again, this time of pioneers and brave young men and women taking to the skies, in fulfilment of either their dreams or the obligations placed upon them.

The Yorkshire Air Museum can be found off the B1228, which is located by taking the A64 York by-pass to the Hull-Bridlington roundabout. Exit via the A1079 Hull road then immediately right to Elvington (B1228), the museum is signposted on the right. The museum is open every weekday from 10.30am until 4.00pm; weekends and Bank Holidays until 5.00pm. In winter times vary so please check on 01904 608246 or contact www.yorksairmuseum.freeserve.co.uk

10. Thomas Cooke : Telescope Maker of York

by Martin Lunn MBE

THOMAS COOKE came from a very humble background, yet nobody could imagine that he would go on to become one of the greatest telescope makers the world has ever seen (Figure 1).

He was born in the village of Allerthorpe in the East Riding of Yorkshire on 8 March 1807. There is little information concerning his early life but we know he attended school for only two years, where he appeared to have average ability. After he finished school Thomas was put to work rather reluctantly in his father's business making and repairing shoes. Thomas quite quickly decided, however, that making shoes was not for him. As a young boy his hero was Captain James Cook of South Seas fame, and he too dreamt of becoming a navigator and exploring the seven seas just has Cook had done the previous century. In his spare time Thomas taught himself navigation, geometry, mathematics and optics. No mean feat for somebody who was only described as being of average ability at school.

At the age of seventeen Cooke, with his bags packed, was ready to depart for Hull and join a ship. However, his mother begged him not to leave and being of a

Figure 1. A portrait of Thomas Cooke.

sensitive nature, he agreed to stay. Unfortunately, the problem Thomas had was that if he remained at home he would need to earn an income, but the prospect of continuing with cobbling did not appeal to him. He reasoned therefore, that if he was good enough to teach himself, he might be able to become a teacher and teach others.

In 1825 at the age of eighteen Thomas opened a school in the nearby village of Bielby. This school was founded for the education of the sons and daughters of wealthy landowners and farmers. Reasonably successful, sometime later he moved his school to Skirpenbeck near Stamford Bridge. It was while teaching in the village that he met Hannah Milner, who was to become his wife.

Cooke later moved to York and continued in teaching from 1829 to 1836. The money he earned allowed him to indulge his leisure interests in practical mechanics and optics. It was at this time that he constructed his first telescope using the thick bottom of a whisky tumbler. This he fashioned into a lens which he then placed into a tube. The telescope was of the finest quality and was bought by John Phillips, who was the first Keeper of the Yorkshire Museum.

Phillips and Cooke enjoyed a very good relationship. Indeed it was John Phillips who was instrumental in the formation of the British Association for the Advancement of Science that held its first meeting in York in 1831. It was Phillips who also encouraged Thomas to keep up his academic interests, so much so, that in March 1837, helped with a loan of £100 from his wife's uncle, Thomas Cooke opened his first optical shop at 50 Stonegate.

One of Cooke's first major orders was for a 4¹/₂-inch refractor telescope for William Gray of York. The Gray family was extremely influential in the city, and the support given by people like these assisted Cooke firmly to establish his business which by 1844 had expanded so much that he was forced to look for larger premises. In addition to making telescopes he was also producing microscopes, opera glasses, spectacles, eye-glasses, optical lenses, single and double barrel air pumps, electrical machines, barometers, thermometers, globes and sundials.

The site he selected was 12 Coney Street. It is important to remember that Cooke was reviving the art of making refracting telescopes, or telescopes with lenses in Britain. In the late eighteenth and early nineteenth centuries the government put a high taxation on the manufacture of flint glass. This resulted in the English trade in optics suffering badly, consequently most of the advances in this field were being made in Europe.

Cooke had close links with the Yorkshire Philosophical Society who were responsible for establishing and building the Yorkshire Museum, with its first Keeper, John Phillips. In the Museum Gardens, the York Observatory was erected as a result of the first meeting of the British Association. It has a rotating roof, believed to be designed by John Smeaton, who designed the Eddystone Lighthouse. The 4¹/₂-inch refracting telescope inside is not the original instrument Thomas Cooke built for the observatory, but

CLOCK CONSTRUCTED FOR DURHAM CATHEDRAL.
TO STRIKE THE HOURS & CHIME THE CAMBRIDGE QUARTERS.

Figure 2. A Cooke turret clock.

another made by him in 1850 and installed in 1981 after a major refurbishment to mark the British Association's 150th anniversary meeting held in York that year.

Apart from observing the moon and planets, the York Observatory was also built to record star positions to determine the time. By 1844 a new transit instrument for measuring the position of the stars to calibrate the time clocks accurately was required at the York Observatory, and Cooke very characteristically donated one.

In 1852 Thomas began manufacturing turret clocks (Figure 2), many of which are found in churches and are often still in use today. These clocks are huge and typically measure in size seven feet high, seven feet long and four feet in breadth and weigh about one ton. Sometimes they were required to show the time on several dials which explains their size.

According to the 1851 census, Cooke employed four men and one apprentice. On the telescope side of the business the firm was receiving orders from all over the country for instruments with lenses

Figure 3. The Buckingham Works in York, built on the site of the 2nd Duke of Buckingham's mansion house.

measuring between 6¹/₂-inch and nine inches. Until then Thomas had concentrated on the British market, in 1855, however, he decided to exhibit at the Universal Exhibition held in Paris. Cooke won a first class medal for a clockwork driven 7¹/₂-inch equatorial telescope. This of course, enhanced his reputation in Europe and meant more orders from abroad.

It was now becoming apparent that the Coney Street works was not large enough to cope with demand, so in the year of the Paris Exhibition, he purchased the site of Duke's Hall, where once stood the home of the second Duke of Buckingham which had long since been demolished. This site became known as the Buckingham Works (Figure 3). It was here that Thomas Cooke set up Britain's first purpose-built telescope making factory. At this period the first change in the Cooke family business took place, with the name changing from Thomas Cooke, York to Thomas Cooke and Sons, York. The earliest known instrument marked 'T. Cooke and Sons, York' is a sundial made in 1857.

By 1861, with the Buckingham Works established, Cooke was employing twenty-six men and fourteen boys all working to a set of rules and regulations that could be quite harsh (Figure 4). Cooke appreciated the importance of having some sort of representation in

London, so between 1863 and 1869 he rented 31 Southampton Street, The Strand. Here people visited the shop, placed their orders, which were then sent to York and the finished article was then transported to the capital.

By this time Thomas' reputation had grown so much that in 1860 he was summoned to Osborne House on the Isle of Wight to receive personally an order from Queen Victoria's husband, HRH the Prince Consort. The instrument made for Prince Albert was described as a 'most elegant' telescope with a 5 1/2-inch lens and a tube six feet long.

At the 1862 London International Exhibition, Cooke had a stand that on the instructions of Her Majesty's Commissioners, was allocated a conspicuous place (Figure 5).

BUCKINGHAM WORKS.
RULES AND REGULATIONS.
FINES.

	s.	d.		s.	d.
1. For smoking in the Works	1	0	15. For leaving work without having carefully extinguished his light	0	6
2. For bringing in malt liquors or spirits during the working hours	1	0	16. For using any stores, such as wood, iron, steel, oil, paint, tallow, candles, or waste improperly, or cutting and using large wood where small would do, or wasting brass turnings	1	0
3. For introducing a stranger into the Works without leave	2	6			
4. Any workman taking chips, tools, or any other thing belonging to his employers, from the premises, otherwise than for the purpose of the business, will be regarded as guilty of felony.			17. For being in any other than his own workship without leave, or sufficient cause	1	0
5. For taking another person's tools without his permission	0	6	18. For handling work not his own	0	6
6. For altering any model, pattern, standard tool or measure, without leave	2	6	19. For picking or breaking any drawer or box lock	2	6
7. For tearing or defacing drawings	1	0	20. For swearing or using indecent language	1	0
8. For neglecting to return to their proper places within a quarter of an hour from the time of having used them, any taps, screw stocks, arbors, or other tools, considered as general tools	0	6	21. Any apprentice absenting himself without leave from Messrs. Cooke or the Clerk, be fined	1	6
9. For injuring a machine or valuable tool, through wantonness or neglect, the cost of repairing it.			22. For writing or sketching anything indecent upon, or defacing any part of the Works, or the Rules, Regulations, or Notices therein fixed up	2	6
10. For striking any person in the Works	2	6	23. For neglecting to hang up his cheque when leaving work, or for losing it	0	6
11. For ordering any tool, smith's work, or castings, without being duly authorized	1	0	24. Windows broken will be charged to the parties working in the same room, unless the person who did the damage be ascertained.		
12. For reading a book or newspaper in the working hours, wasting time in unnecessary conversation or otherwise, or whistling	0	6	25. Boys' fines to be only one half, except the Rule which applies to the breaking of windows; in which case the full amount will be levied.		
13. For washing, putting on his coat, or making any other preparation of a similar kind for leaving work before the appointed time	0	6	26. That every man sweep and make tidy his bench or lathe every Saturday commencing not before ten minutes to One.		
14. For neglecting after his day's work is done to note down correctly on his time slate the various jobs he may have been engaged upon during the day, with the time for each job	0	6	☞ The above Fines and Regulations are intended solely for the purpose of maintaining better order in the Works, preventing wasteful and unnecessary expense, and for promoting the good conduct and respectability of the workmen.		

August, 1865. **T. COOKE & SONS.**

LANCASTER PRINTER, YORK.

Figure 4. Rules and Regulations.

Figure 5. Cooke's stand at the London International Exhibition, 1862.

Among the telescopes on display was an eight-inch refractor with a brass tube twelve feet long, considered even by Cooke as a most elegant instrument. Together with this telescope there were other smaller equatorial telescopes, some transit instruments, a turret clock, plus other goods including a turning lathe, a screw cutting lathe and a wheel-cutting engine.

Another exhibitor at the 1862 London Exhibition were the Chance Brothers, of Birmingham, who were glass manufacturers. They had produced two glass discs, each one measuring twenty-five inches across. Robert Newall of Gateshead, who had grown wealthy from the production of wire-rope bought these glass discs for £500 each.

Figure 6. The Newall telescope completed in 1869 and seen here about 1870.

Figure 7. Thomas Cooke's steam carriage dating from about 1866.

He asked Thomas Cooke if he could construct a telescope using them. Cooke accepted the challenge, but he badly miscalculated the costs involved and the time it would take to build the telescope. He had anticipated producing it in about twelve months. In fact it took six years and was actually completed one year after Cooke's death. When finished in 1869, the Newall Refracting Telescope which had a lens twenty-five inches across, a tube thirty-two feet in length and weighed nine tons was the largest telescope in the world (Figure 6).

After its completion the telescope remained at Gateshead until the end of the nineteenth century when it was transferred to Cambridge, then in 1957 it was relocated to the Greek National Observatory in Athens where it is still in use today.

It was well-known that Thomas Cooke had a very fertile mind and in time he invented many different types of equipment. Cooke had a brother Barnard, living in Hull, and Thomas was not very impressed with the stagecoach service between Hull and York. Working in 1866 with one of his sons, Charles Frederick, he built a steam carriage in order to make the journey between Hull and York quicker (Figure 7). The steam carriage appears to have existed from about 1866 until 1872. Unfortunately, however, under the law at that period it was stated that any vehicle that was not pulled by a horse had to have a man with a red flag walking in front of the vehicle. This, of course, limited the speed of the vehicle to the pace of a man, about four miles an hour! The steam carriage invented by Thomas had a speed of about fifteen miles per hour, naturally it broke the speed limit! In addition, at least one appears to have crashed injuring some of the occupants. As a result of these obstacles, steam carriages were eventually dismantled and taken off the road.

Thomas Cooke died in 1868 at the age of sixty-one. It is said he literally worked himself into his grave. After his untimely death the business was carried on by his two sons - Charles Frederick Cooke was the engineer and Thomas Cooke, junior, was an optician. In his will Thomas left everything to his wife Hannah. However, Robert Newall was still unhappy with the financial arrangements concerning his yet unfinished telescope and at one stage endeavoured to force Cooke's widow and her sons into liquidation. The enterprise was saved from bankruptcy by the wealthy industrialist Sir James Meek, who was three times Lord Mayor of York. He bought and then sold the business to Thomas Cooke's old friend James Wigglesworth.

Wigglesworth entered into a partnership with Cooke's sons in 1879. When he died in 1888 he left his share in the Buckingham Works to his son Robert, who remained a partner until the business became a limited company in 1897. The twenty-five years following Thomas Cooke's death saw his sons continue the tradition in designing and constructing many notable instruments.

Until the 1860s the London-based firm Troughton and Simms were the principal suppliers of optical equipment to the East India Company. This changed in the early 1870s. In 1872 Cooke and Sons supplied the specially built transit telescopes for the great trigonometrical survey of India. Initially there were some technical problems, but when these had been resolved, the great survey of the Indian continent was carried out successfully.

In 1885 a major civil engineering construction was begun in Scotland, when the Forth Road Bridge was built over the Firth of Forth. Naturally, the surveyors engaged on the project required the best theodolites available to position the bridge accurately. Cookes were asked to build special theodolites that were described when completed as 'excellent' and 'practically indestructible'.

Although optical equipment continued to be the mainstay of the

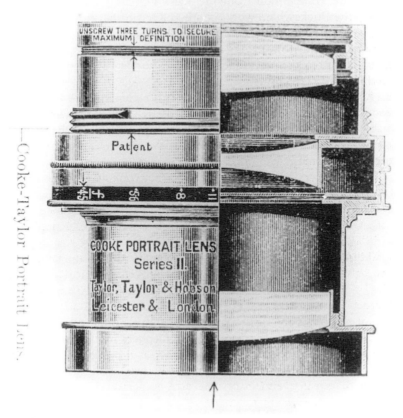

Figure 8. Cooke Portrait Lens.

business, with their experience of telescope construction, they began to undertake the erection of observatory roofs or domes. It is said that they were the first to use papier-mâché rather than the heavier copper cladding which had been previously favoured. In 1883 the firm produced the famous dome for the Greenwich Observatory which became known as the 'onion dome' because of its construction. Over the following years they supplied domes to observatories across the globe including that at the Cape of Good Hope in South Africa and the Royal Observatories at Brussels, Liège and Sofia together with observatories in Madras, Odessa and Rio de Janeiro.

At the end of the nineteenth century industry in Britain fell into decline. In addition there were problems arising from the recent unification of the German states when their companies began to make inroads into traditionally British markets. For Cooke and Sons this meant competition from the Zeiss Optical Company. Never-theless the Buckingham Works continued to prosper not least by the involvement of Harold Dennis Taylor who had joined the firm in 1882 and quickly proved himself a brilliant and inventive young man. He soon rose to become Optical Manager and in 1895 took a seat on the Board of Directors.

H.D. Taylor's great contribution to optics came in 1893 when he designed and built the Cooke Portrait Lens (Figure 8). This lens is made up of three elements and removed much of the colour distortion that had caused problems in earlier telescopes. At one stroke the company had taken another giant leap forward in the field of optics. Others followed suit in producing triple lenses, but it was Cookes who were first. It should perhaps be pointed out that almost every modern telescope, camera or piece of optical equipment that has a triplet lens, can trace its history back to the Buckingham Works in 1893.

With colour distortion virtually overcome and with the advent of photography the astronomer John Franklin Adams conceived of the idea of a photographic survey of the night sky. Using Cooke telescopes and cameras he began the project in 1902 and finished two years later. The Northern Hemisphere was photographed from Godalming in Surrey, the Southern Hemisphere from Cape Town in South Africa. The Franklin Adams Survey as it became known, was the standard reference for astronomers throughout most of the twentieth century, and even now astronomers still refer to these charts.

One of the reasons that the company remained successful for so many years was because they made sure that they had offices throughout the British Empire. If optical equipment was required by surveyors, for whatever purpose, gold or silver prospecting for instance, the local representative would be contacted who would then pass the order on to York who would ship the items out as soon as possible. Some idea of the increased costs involved in sending optical instruments out to different parts of the Empire can be seen in the following figures. In 1899 a four-inch theodolite cost £28 in York, £33 in Cape Town and £42 10s 0d in Johannesburg.

The British Antarctic explorer Robert Scott attempted to become the first person to reach the South Pole. Tragically he and his companions died on the expedition in 1912 which failed in its attempt, being beaten by the Norwegian Amundsen. Scott needed to measure accurately the position of the South Pole, and so Cookes were asked to construct six special lightweight theodolites for the expedition.

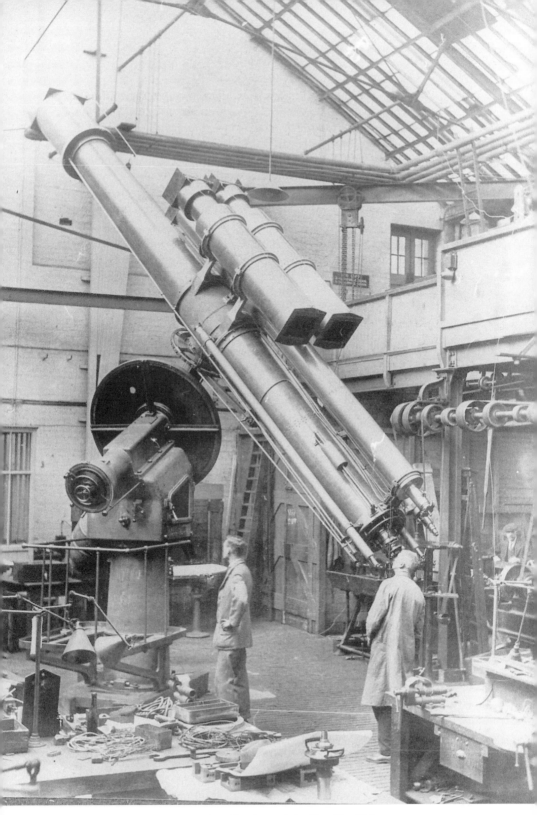

Figure 9. The Buckingham Works and the Brazilian Telescope.

With the coming of the First World War, through the trading firm Argo set up in 1908, Cookes sold range-finders to navies throughout the world. In addition to the Royal Navy, the navies of Brazil, Chile, France, Greece, Italy, and the United States of America all had Argo-Cooke range-finders. An order for the Austro-Hungarian Navy was cancelled at the commencement of hostilities.

During the early part of the First World War the range-finders of the Royal Navy ships were not as accurate as the Zeiss range-finders on the German warships. In response to this the Navy requested the best person in the country to go to Scapa Flow in Scotland where the fleet was based to re-calibrate the instruments so that the guns would hit their targets. The best person for the task was E. Wilfred Taylor, the son of H.D. Taylor, who was serving as a colonel in the Royal Artillery on the Western Front. He went to Scapa Flow during 1914-15 and from warship to warship he re-calibrated the naval range-finders.

The Buckingham Works was turned over to the production of munitions from 1915 until the end of the war, during which period, as with many other factories of this nature, the work was undertaken by women. At this time too, there were changes within the firm. In 1915 the Vickers Company took a 70 per cent holding in Cookes. In 1920 Cookes took a controlling interest in Troughton and Simms, and two years later the company Cooke, Troughton and Simms was formed with its head office in York.

Following the war and the years of change, Cookes retained a full order book. In 1921 the Shackleton-Rowett expedition to the Antarctic used Cooke theodolites because, as in the previous expedition to these polar regions, Cookes' instruments were still considered the best. There were still large telescope orders. Brazil ordered a telescope with a lens measuring eighteen inches across, which was delivered in 1923 (Figure 9). The entire telescope and mechanism weighed about eight tons. In addition to supplying the instrument, the company also built the dome for the observatory at Rio de Janeiro.

The 1930s witnessed the great depression both here and abroad. Cookes were affected just as other industrial companies. Nevertheless the Royal Greenwich Observatory approached Cookes to construct a new transit instrument. However, from the very beginning it was obvious that there were problems, not least was the calibre of craftsmen available to undertake the project. With financial problems the firm had laid off many older skilled workmen. This was to prove a costly and short-sighted error. When the transit instrument

Figure 10. The Haxby Road Works.

was finished in 1936 it was found to be unsatisfactory. In the following year it was returned to York for extra work which itself was never completed satisfactorily. Even as late as 1941-42 the Astronomer Royal, Harold Spencer Jones was complaining that the transit telescope was not performing as expected. From this commission Cookes took the decision not to undertake the construction of any further large individual instruments, as they were not profitable. Indeed, in the summer of 1938 Cookes sold off their astronomical side of the business to Grubb Parsons Limited of Newcastle.

Ironically, the previous year Cookes had begun to look for bigger premises to replace the old Buckingham Works. A new factory in Haxby Road was erected in 1939 (Figure 10). This new manufactory was large enough to accommodate 1,000 men, whereas the old Buckingham Works had had space for seven hundred. The Buckingham Works remained empty from 1939 and was eventually sold off in 1948 to the North-Eastern Electricity Board. It has since been demolished to be replaced by residential housing.

The outbreak of the Second World War saw Haxby Road being commandeered for the production of optical equipment for the war effort. By 1942 40 per cent of the workforce was made up of female operatives. Towards the end of hostilities civil orders began to predominate again; the postwar prospects looked good for the company with vast amounts of scientific, surveying and engineering equipment being required to replace what had been lost during the war years.

Today, only a small fraction of the Haxby Road site is still employed in the production of optical equipment, not by the firm of Thomas Cooke, but by a company called Bio-Rad who specialise in the building of precision instruments for use in microchip technology. The name Thomas Cooke and Sons of York was finally amalgamated into the Vickers Instrument Company, and our story ends when Thomas Cooke ceased to be a trading name on 1 January 1963.

11. The Walls and Bars of York

by Alan Whitworth

THE WALLS OF YORK enclosing the old city are probably the most complete and certainly the finest of any surviving medieval town walls in England (Figure 1). Their value to York cannot be overstated. Since the establishment of Eboracum as an important military settlement during the Roman period the defences have been progressively enlarged and refined; until today, in their final form, they stand as perhaps the most vital feature of its history and character.

There can be little doubt that notwithstanding the magnificence of York's streets, buildings and the Minster, it is its walls that create the most immediate and lasting impression of this city in the minds of visitors. Certainly when first viewed either in spring, with the ramparts bedecked in daffodils, or at night floodlit against a dark sky, their effect can be quite breathtaking.

The whole of the walls extending for over two miles is in the ownership of the City Council and so, for the most part, is the massive earth bank on which they sit together with the adjacent defensive ditches.

The first Roman fortress, which was founded in AD71, extended

Figure 1. York Minster and the city walls.

over an area of about fifty acres and was enclosed by an open ditch backed by a low earth bank and timber palisade. This area was bounded on its northern side by the line of the present walls along Gillygate and Lord Mayor's Walk and on its southern side by King's Square, Feasegate, and along the rear of Coney Street. At various times during the Roman occupation the defences were modified and enlarged, until in the fourth century the military fortress was totally enclosed by a stone wall about six metres in height. The civilian town on the south side of the river Ouse had also by this date been enclosed by a defensive wall.

After the departure of the Romans in AD 410 the walls began to fall into decay from neglect. During the 'Dark Ages' that followed there seems to have been little or no major refortification and the Anglian defenders of York presumably manned the crumbling Roman walls and plugged any breaches with timber or stonework, as in the case of the Anglian Tower. Any further actual improvements or modifications to the walls did not appear to have taken place until the time of the Danish occupation of the city in AD 867, when an improved rampart surmounted by a timber breastwork was, in all probability constructed .

During the eleventh century the Norman 'conquerors' extended the line of the defences to enclose an altogether much larger area of 263 acres which is more or less the area of the present walled city. They raised the rampart to a new height probably using soil from the city ditch that was apparently widened and deepened, and erected a new massive timber breastwork on top of this. The two castles, one on each bank of the river, were also built but that on the south bank known as the 'Castle of the Old Baile' had only a very short life before falling into disuse. It was during this period that the river Foss was dammed to create a large impassable expanse of water known as the 'King's Fishpond' - now the Foss Island district - which obviated the need for the construction of any defensive structure between Layerthorpe Tower and the Red Tower.

The rampart was finally increased in height to its present level in the thirteenth century. This was about one metre higher than the Norman bank and about three metres above the top of the Roman wall. It was surmounted initially by a timber breastwork that was then later replaced by the present stone wall. The full length of the perimeter defences, which include open stretches of water and some now demolished wall, extends to about two and three-quarter miles.

In subsequent centuries the defences played a prominent part in protecting the citizens from incursions by the Scots from the 'North' during the wars with Scotland and in the Civil War when the city came under siege in 1644.

The original wall ran from a circular water tower at the side of the Ouse up to Baile Hill. The postern gateway adjacent to this water tower was removed illegally by the City Council in 1807 and the tower itself, together with the remaining walling were demolished seventy years later. The city wall therefore now begins at Baile Hill or to be exact at the adjacent tower from which a flight of steps, overhung by trees on Baile Hill, leads up to the 'Wall Walk'.

For most of its length the wall between Baile Hill and Victoria Bar enclosed the bailey or open ground of the 'Castle of the Old Baile'. When the castle fell into disuse the land passed in the thirteenth century to the Archbishop of York and substantial evidence of masons' marks on the walls in this area suggests that the Minster masons may well have been employed on maintenance or rebuilding work hereabouts. Between towers (three) and (five) there is also an extensive area of brickwork incorporated at some time into repairs to the wall.

Between the start of the wall and Victoria Bar there are six towers.

Tower one at the base of the walls at Baile Hill was constructed in 1878, after the removal of the wall up from the river. It is semi-octagonal in form and Victorian in character. It has crenallations around the wall tops that are built of brown sandstone quite out of keeping with the remainder of the walls. In the nineteenth century the removal of any part of the city wall seems to have been accompanied by the construction at the wall break of a public urinal. Accordingly there is attached to this tower a stone public urinal apparently erected at the same time and now closed.

Tower two is midway along the stretch of wall overlooking Bishopgate Street and is semi-circular in plan, measuring five metres wide and extending just over two metres beyond the wall face. It appears to have been independently constructed from the wall and is now filled in.

Tower three, also known as Birchdaughter Tower, stands at the wall angle overlooking the busy junction of Price's Lane and Bishopgate Street. The tower is circular in shape and the rampart on its outer face is hereabouts very high and steep. It was probably rebuilt in the seventeenth century and appears to have been used for a number of purposes including that of a cowshed in the nineteenth century. It has a brick arched roof to the chamber below.

Tower four is semi-circular. It is five metres wide and projects nearly three metres from the wall surface. At some period it has been filled.

Tower five is substantial, measuring over seven metres in width and projecting over three metres from the wall face. It is demi-hexagonal in form and appears to have been filled.

Tower six appears to have been a later addition to the wall defences. It is rectangular in plan, measuring five metres by just two metres.

Victoria Bar is a relatively simple opening through the city wall and was constructed in 1838 to provide a link between the city and the increasing development without in the Nunnery Lane area. It comprises a single arch span of twelve feet over Victoria Street. The two side arches for pedestrian access were added in 1864 and 1877. There is a commemorative plaque set into the wall above the central arch that reads:

> *Erected by Public Subscription under the direction of the City Commissioner AD1838. George Hudson, Esq, Lord Mayor.*

From immediately before Victoria Bar to Micklegate Bar the wall changes in character suggesting the building was of a different period to the preceding section. The inner wall supporting the 'Wall Walk' was constructed during the nineteenth century restoration of the walls but the outer original face is of smaller sized ashlar blocks laid mostly in straight courses with the surmounting parapet set slightly back from the outer wall face. In general, the construction of this section is poor without proper foundations. The wall sits on a steeply graded part of the rampart.

Tower seven, known as Sadler Tower, is D-shaped in form projecting two metres in front of the wall and one metre behind it. It has a stone vaulted roof. This tower is thought to be one of the oldest surviving interval towers in the entire defences. It has been subject to some adaptations over the years and a brick fireplace has been inserted at some later date. During the 1970s the wooden door was replaced with a metal grill.

Tower eight is rectangular and measures nearly six metres wide while standing one metre proud of the wall face. It appears to have been added later to the wall although since its original erection it may possibly have been subject to considerable reconstruction making its dating difficult. The construction of the tower is very poor by comparison to other towers that have been added later.

Tower nine is again D-shape in plan extending about two metres in front of the wall and one metre behind it. It has a stone vaulted roof supporting the walkway platform but was probably much higher originally.

Tower ten is filled in. Rectangular in plan it measures some four

Figure 2. Micklegate Bar from Micklegate.

metres wide and stands one metre proud of the wall.

Tower eleven is semi-circular in shape, projecting two metres from the wall face and measuring four metres in diameter. It has been filled in. The tower is supported by a quite substantial base.

Micklegate Bar was the main gateway into York from London and the south-west (Figure 2). It was therefore the most important of the four major entrances and has consequently been the scene of much pageantry including the arrival of the present Queen Elizabeth II on her visits to the city in 1971 and 1977. In earlier centuries the heads of traitors and rebels were displayed on the Bar and here were exposed the heads of Lord Scrope, of Masham, in 1415; the head of Richard, Duke of York, after the battle of Wakefield, 1460, facing inwards *so York may overlook York* (Shakespeare, 3 Henry IV, Pt 4); the Earl of Northumberland, in 1572, and many others, the last being the Jacobite rebels William Connolly and James Mayne, in 1746.

Its date of erection is between 1196 and 1230, on older foundations. The structure contains a Norman arched gate constructed in the twelfth century and a three-storey superstructure added in the early fourteenth century. The floors and roof are of timber and the Bar contains two turrets on its outer side rising from the second floor level. This is the only Bar to have a hipped and slated roof.

A timber and plaster extension similar to that at Walmgate Bar was

Figure 3. Micklegate Bar.

probably added in Elizabethan times but this was removed and the present inner face constructed in 1827 to the design of architect Peter Atkinson (1776-1842). The Barbican, already in a dilapidated state, was removed in 1826. The side arches for foot and vehicular traffic are also a nineteenth century addition.

On the 16 July 1644 the Royalists surrendered the city (after three months of siege) to the besieging Parliamentary forces at this point. Although Micklegate Bar did not appear to suffer much damage during the siege of York since then it has been subject to frequent restoration and repair work. The last major restoration was in 1952. The stone figures on top of the Bar date from this time and are not antiquities (Figure 3). In 1968 the west turret was completely dismantled to roof level and rebuilt. The heraldry, comprising the Royal Arms and the shields of York City and Sir John Lister-Kaye, was repainted and refurbished in 1979.

The wall between Micklegate Bar and Tofts Tower at the west angle of the defences seems to have been rebuilt at various periods. As far as tower (twelve) the inner face was probably rebuilt in the nineteenth century but the remainder is clearly of much earlier date. The outer face is extensively supported by a series of stone buttresses.

From Tofts Tower at the angle the wall rises and falls as it runs down to Barker Tower at the Ouse. This length of wall has been pierced in a number of places with arched openings, some to provide access to the old railway station within the walled area, and some to the later present station outside. The two older arches nearer Tofts Tower were formed in 1840 (north) and 1845 (south). Station Road Arch giving access to the new station was erected in 1874 and Lendal Arch two years later.

Lendal Arch, like Station Road Arch, originally had a road arch with two side pedestrian arches. It was raised in height in 1909 to accommodate trams and completely reconstructed in 1965 as a single span, formed of cranked steel beams with stone cladding. Station Road Arch was extensively repaired in 1968 and again in 1976.

Between Micklegate Bar and Barker Tower (Figure 4) there are six interval towers commencing with tower twelve which is rectangular in form measuring a little over three metres in width and projecting nearly two metres from the wall face. This tower has been filled in.

Tower thirteen known as Tofts Tower, stands at the west angle of the defences. It is rectangular in plan and about six metres wide and eight metres

Figure 4. Barker Tower from North Street.

in length. It has a single chamber with a brick vaulted roof supporting the walkway and platform over. The tower was possibly rebuilt in 1745 after being partially demolished by the Scots the previous year and has been subject to later adaptations.

Tower fourteen is demi-hexagonal in form and projects out about one metre from the wall face. It has been substantially incorporated into a rebuild of the wall at this point and undoubtedly was less so originally.

Tower fifteen is very close to tower fourteen and is rectangular in plan. It measures approximately five metres wide and projects nearly two metres from the wall face. It is in part supported by a buttress on the outer rampart side, but this may have already been in existence before the tower was put up. Again the tower is filled in.

Tower sixteen is demi-hexagonal and although apparently partly rebuilt above plinth level, it is thought to be little altered since it was first erected about the fourteenth century. The chamber has a brick vaulted roof and a window opening has been formed around the outer arrow slit.

Tower seventeen stands close to the Station Road Arch and is again demi-hexagonal in plan projecting nearly two metres from the wall face and measuring three metres in width. The plinth is stepped at the sides and the parapet which was rebuilt in 1832 is also set back from the wall face. The tower is now solid.

Tower eighteen was situated at the site of Lendal Arch and disappeared when the original arch was constructed in 1876.

Barker Tower stands at the river's edge and is now more generally

Figure 5. Barker Tower submerged under the flooded river Ouse, 1991.

known as North Street Postern Tower, or occasionally as the 'Dead House' on account of it having been used at the end of the nineteenth century as a mortuary for bodies pulled out of the water (Figure 5). When constructed in the fourteenth century this little circular tower was a single storey building with a flat roof but in the seventeenth century the present timber and tiled conical roof was added to the parapet creating a second, upper storey. A chain was slung across the river between this tower and a corresponding 'watch' tower on the opposite bank that could be raised and lowered to control trading ships from entering the city without paying tolls (Figure 6). Until the building of Lendal Bridge it was let to a ferryman who operated a ferry across the river Ouse at this point.

In the early part of the nineteenth century a brick house was added to Barker Tower but this was removed in 1840. In more recent years, the building was used for a time by the York City Parks Department until it was extensively restored in 1970.

The wall from Lendal Tower to Bootham Bar is a hotch-potch of isolated stretches representing nearly all stages of the development of the defences. No part of this section of the 'Wall Walk, however, is open to the public.

From Lendal Tower the wall rises steeply up Lendal Hill to the ruins of St Leonard's Hospital, where it joins the line of the original Roman fortress wall. This stretch now ends at the lodge of the gateway into the Museum Gardens, and has been subject to extensive nineteenth century modification and reconstruction. From St Leonard's Hospital to the Multangular Tower the wall is almost entirely Roman although there has been later patching and the total clearance of the medieval rampart within which it was probably buried at one time.

From the Multangular Tower the wall divides into two separate lengths. The medieval wall stands on the outer side of the earlier Roman wall and is now supported on a concrete and cobbled base, its inner rampart having been partly removed in 1969 to expose a buried Anglian tower and surviving Roman works. The outer rampart along King's Manor Lane was refurbished in 1971. The exposed Roman wall stands to a height of approximately two metres with well preserved outer facing masonry and parts of its tiled course surviving.

Figure 6. Across the river Ouse to Lendal Water Tower.

This Roman section contains the remains of one interval tower and beyond this towards St Leonard's Place has a later 'Dark Ages' tower known as the Anglian Tower incorporated into it. A further short length of Roman wall survives in the City Council car park and another short section is preserved in the basement of the public toilets near Bootham Bar.

Immediately beyond the Anglian Tower the inner rampart has been cut back in section in a series of steps revealing the progressive stages of development of the earth banks. At this point there is a break in the medieval wall up to Bootham Bar, created when St Leonard's Place was formed in the 1830s.

Lendal Tower was originally a small water tower similar to Barker Tower on the opposite bank and between the two was slung a chain. This tower has almost entirely been rebuilt and considerably enlarged to accommodate pumping machinery for York's water supply (Figure 7). The initial alterations were made in the early part of the seventeenth century but further work followed to both the tower and its machinery in subsequent centuries.

The Multangular Tower stands at the west angle of the old Roman fortress (Figure 8). It is now a combination of both original Roman and later medieval construction. The lower six metres of wall is of Roman walling to which above a further three metres of medieval wall has been added. The tower is impressive and substantial in appearance measuring thirteen metres across and comprising nine short stretches of wall each about three metres long; hence its name 'multangular'. It stands to a height of nine metres although up to one

Figure 7. A nineteenth century engraving of Lendal Tower Waterworks.

hundred and fifty years ago it had been filled in almost up to the base of its upper medieval section.

The outer rampart restarts at the western side of the tower, rising up towards the continuation of the medieval wall leading in the direction of Bootham Bar.

Tower nineteen, known as the Anglian Tower, is constructed in a breach of the Roman wall and has no direct attachment to the adjacent medieval wall of later date. The existence of this tower was rediscovered in 1838 when a tunnel was cut through the rampart to

Figure 8. The Multangular Tower.

link stables on the inner side of the wall to the open area outside. No substantial excavation was undertaken, however, until 1969, when the tower and adjacent Roman wall were investigated by Mr Jeffrey Radley, who was tragically killed during a subsequent archaeological examination of the site.

The Anglian Tower is square in plan with an arch roof and is constructed of oolithic limestone quite different from that of any other part of the defences. It is thought to have been built about AD700, and is believed to be unique. There may have been at least one storey above the single chamber that now remains. The vaulted roof has been substantially replaced with brick probably in the nineteenth century.

The tower and adjacent Roman wall were extensively restored and consolidated in 1970 when the entire area was opened out for permanent public display; the project was the subject of a subsequent Civic Trust National Award for excellence.

Bootham Bar (Figure 9) is the only Bar to stand on the site of one of the original Roman gateways and was the principal entrance into the city from Scotland and the north-west through the Forest of Galtres, and as such it played a prominent part during the wars with Scotland. Armed guides were stationed here to conduct travellers through the forest and protect them from attack by wolves. The Royal Arms were taken down in 1650 when Oliver Cromwell passed through on his way to attack Scotland. In 1663, the heads of three rebels were exposed on the Bar for passing seditious comment against the restored monarchy. Parts of the present structure date from the twelfth century but some of the stone is almost certainly reused stone from the earlier Roman gate which had formerly stood on the site. The upper two storeys were added in the fourteenth century, but have seen much adaptation and remodelling, particularly in 1719 and 1889 when at the latter date a way through was provided for the public to gain access to the walls.

There are two outer bartizans and, unlike on any of the other Bars, there are also two inner bartizans. These were added during the nineteenth century reconstruction of the inner façade, presumably for aesthetic reasons. A portcullis remains too. The barbican was removed in 1832 when St Leonard's Place was formed and at this date the Bar itself was saved from complete demolition only as result of a public outcry by the citizens of York.

Restoration work was carried out to Bootham Bar in 1951 but substantial cracking and settlement began to occur ten years later and in 1969 the whole structure was underpinned by means of the

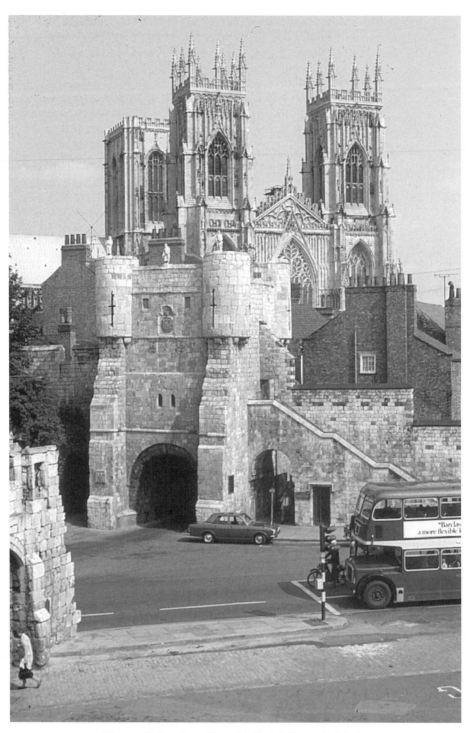

Figure 9. Bootham Bar with York Minster behind.

insertion of 106 needle piles through the lower part of the structure. At this time also a system of stainless steel tie bars was incorporated within the walls to encircle the building at two floor levels. Both this and the system of piling are thought to have been employed here for the first time on any ancient monument in this country.

The walls between Bootham Bar and Robin Hood's Tower are flanked on their outer side by the private back gardens of properties along Gillygate and on the inner side by the Dean's garden and other property managed by the Dean and Chapter of York Minster. This length of 'Wall Walk' together with the adjacent length of walk to Monk Bar is probably the finest of any part of the defences and has been described as one of the finest town walks in Europe.

The walkway, now mostly supported on arches was largely reconstructed in 1889 by Edwin Gray (who later served as Lord Mayor in 1898) when this length of wall (thirty-seven Linear Yards) was the first section opened to the public. The parapet was also reconstructed at this time.

Tower twenty-two has a raised platform reached by a number of steps up from the 'Wall Walk'. It is demi-hexagonal in form, some five metres wide and projecting a little over two metres from the wall face.

Tower twenty-three is also raised above the level of the 'Wall Walk'. This is demi-hexagonal in plan projecting two metres from the wall face and is five metres wide. The tower appears to have been subject to some modification and has a brick vaulted roof. It is open to the rear.

Tower twenty-four is similar in form to the two previous again with a raised platform but projecting nearly three metres from the wall face. The interior has a brick and stone arch roof and the tower is now open to the rear.

Tower twenty-five is semi-circular, five metres wide and projects nearly two metres from the wall face. It has a brick arch roof and brick side walls which were presumably constructed during the 1889 rebuilding work.

Tower twenty-six is semi-circular and similar in form to tower twenty-five although with a larger open chamber. This tower was almost entirely rebuilt after a collapse in 1957.

Tower twenty-seven stands at the wall angle at the junction of Lord Mayor's Walk and Gillygate. This tower is generally known as Robin Hood's Tower although it had been known earlier by a variety of titles including Bawing Tower and Frost Tower in the fifteenth century.

The present structure is relatively modern having been entirely constructed in 1889. It is circular in plan and is sub-divided into two rooms by a modern brick wall. The smaller rear room is roofed by a series of brick and steel jack arches supporting the 'Wall Walk'. The main room has a concrete slab roof supported on steel and concrete beams and modern brick piers.

The city walls from Robin Hood's Tower to Monk Bar follows the line of the north-east wall of the original Roman fortress. As with the Gillygate stretch it probably contains part at least of the old Roman wall buried within its rampart. The substantial outer ditch along Lord Mayor's Walk is the most impressive of any part of the defences and is probably the best preserved medieval ditch remaining in England. The wall for much of its length is supported by external buttresses. On its inner side the rampart has been considerably cut away to accommodate the gardens of private residences mostly in the ownership of St John's College and the Minster authorities.

The inner wall face incorporates a great deal of brickwork probably the result of the nineteenth century rebuilding. There were also a number of stepped accesses up to the 'Wall Walk' from the gardens below but these in general have been rendered unuseable or secured by a locked gate. The north-east gateway of the original Roman fortress was incorporated within this length but there is now no trace of it except for a depression in the rampart opposite Groves Lane which marks the site.

Tower twenty-eight is the only surviving interval tower along this entire section. It is semi-circular in plan measuring approximately four metres wide and projecting two metres from the wall face.

Figure 10. A nineteenth century engraving of Monk Bar.

Although the lower part of this tower appears to be original the upper part was rebuilt in 1889 with small turrets added on each side producing a structure Victorian in character. Internally, the tower contains brick arches supported on concrete beams with some stone flagging to carry the platform.

Tower twenty-nine was completely removed in the early nineteenth century. A depression in the outer rampart indicates where this tower was probably sited.

Monk Bar was the principal gateway into York from the north-east, and is on a line with the Roman wall (Figure 10). Erected as a three-storey structure, with a barbican in the early fourteenth century of magnesium limestone, it replaces an earlier medieval gate which probably stood on the site of the *porta decumana* of the Roman legionary fortress, one hundred yards to the north-east along Lord Mayor's Walk. The fourth uppermost storey was added in the following century. Monk Bar is the tallest of all the Bars standing nearly twenty metres in height and architecturally is certainly the most interesting. It is probably so named after the monks of a neighbouring monastery, and not as erroneously supposed after General Monk, in 1660.

All floors apart from the roof have stone vaulted ceilings. The roof is of timber with lead covering. There are two bartizans the lower rooms of which were once used as the Freemen's Prison (sixteenth century). Variously it has also been used as a house (fifteenth century), a police inspector's residence (nineteenth century) and a scout room (twentieth century). The six stone figures on the outer parapets looking outward towards Monkgate are seventeenth century replacements but are the oldest and most splendid and fearsome of those on any of the Bars. The portcullis remains in good condition though now inoperable it still retains its original windlass to wind it up.

Part of the barbican was removed in 1815 and the remainder in 1825 when side arches were added; that on the south-east side subsequently

Figure 11. Monk Bar and the city walls.

being replaced with the present high road arch in 1861. The Bar was fairly extensively restored in 1952-1953.

Between 1977 and 1978 it became necessary to dismantle the bartizan at the north corner to third floor level and rebuild it with new reinforced concrete floors to provide a better anchorage. The north-east corner bartizan together with the whole of the parapet was dismantled to roof level and a reinforced ring beam incorporated into the rebuilt masonry to provide a hidden belt around the whole of the structure. In conjunction with this work, a partial rebuilding and general repairs were carried out to the lower level of masonry and the heraldry comprising the Royal Arms on the outer face was refurbished and the whole Bar cleaned. The total cost of this was £39,710.

The walls between Monk Bar and the wall end at Layerthorpe have been subject to much adaptation and rebuilding (Figure 11). Their line more or less coincides with the original Roman wall for a distance of some one hundred metres to the Roman Angle Tower that partly survives immediately adjacent to the present wall. From tower thirty-one the wall veers a course toward the south-east as far as tower thirty-two which probably represented the extent of the Danish defences. From this point there is an abrupt change of direction towards the river Foss that was the result of a modified realignment during the Norman period.

The 'Wall Walk' throughout this entire section is supported partly on arches some of which are clearly nineteenth century, but some of which are considerably older. There is also considerable evidence of wall heightening, reconstruction and obvious in-filling of some sections that have collapsed. There are a number of buttresses near the Ice House (early nineteenth century) on the outer rampart which were largely rebuilt in about 1971. The railings between towers thirty-two andthirty-four were added to the 'Wall Walk' in 1978.

Tower thirty originally stood about fifteen metres from the Roman Angle Tower on the Monk Bar side but has now completely disappeared in subsequent rebuilding.

Tower thirty-one known as Harlot Hill Tower was substantially rebuilt in the nineteenth century although the lower masonry may well be original. It is semi-circular in plan measuring about six metres in width. A small bartizan is constructed on each side of the tower at its junction with the wall. The interior of the tower contains a brick vaulted roof.

Tower thirty-two stands at the angle where the probable Norman realignment was introduced. This tower is oval shape in form about seven metres by six metres in size. Substantial strengthening works were carried out to this tower in 1951. The earlier brick vaulting of the chamber was then in a state of collapse and was replaced with a flat reinforced concrete slab. The tower walls were then completely underpinned, and the masonry generally made good.

Tower thirty-three is rectangular and stands at a point where the wall drops in level to within only a few yards of the Jewbury roadway. The tower is five metres wide and stands two metres proud of the wall face. It is now solid and may always have been so.

Tower thirty-four stands close to tower thirty-three and only a few feet from the roadway. This tower is of unusual shape and construction being supported on

Figure 12. The Red Tower.

buttresses which rise from the adjacent street level. These were probably a later addition to the tower that appears to have been subject to considerable modification since its original erection.

The wall between the Red Tower and tower thirty-five is relatively low and for its first fifteen metres or so is virtually level. Beyond this it rises in a series of steps with the introduction of the rampart which presumably rose up out of the King's Fishpond. The wall appears to have been largely rebuilt probably in the mid-nineteenth century and the walkway is now supported for much of its length on segmental arches.

Between towers thirty-five and thirty-six the wall is a continuation

Figure 13. A nineteenth century engraving of Layerthorpe Postern Tower and the old Layerthorpe Bridge, both now demolished.

Its outer wall is supported on an arched foundation. The tower has been filled in, probably during the nineteenth century rebuilding.

Tower thirty-six is a rectangular tower measuring five metres wide and projecting one metre out from the wall face. Again it was filled in during the nineteenth century reconstruction. There appears at some period to have been an opening in the walkway with evidence of steps leading down from the wall on each side of the tower.

Walmgate Bar formed the principal entrance into the city from the south-east (Figure 14). It was originally a stone arched gateway through the timber-palisaded rampart. The original arch dating from the twelfth century is now incorporated into the present Bar, the upper two storeys and barbican of magnesium limestone having been added to it in the following two centuries. A timber and plaster extension supported on Roman-Doric columns was added in the sixteenth century to the inner side of the Bar to provide residential accommodation (Figure 15). The small foot arch to the south-west was put through in 1840 and the large vehicular arch to the north-east in 1862 being an enlargement of an earlier pedestrian archway.

The Bar suffered fire damage at the hands of rebels in 1489 and came in for prolonged heavy canon bombardment from Parliamentary forces situated on Lamel Hill during the Siege of York in the Civil War. It was subsequently extensively rebuilt in 1648 and again substantially repaired in 1840 when considerable rebuilding was necessary to the barbican and a stone plaque records this fact. The money for this work was provided from the £500 paid by the Great North of England Railway to the Corporation for rights of access at North Street Postern to their riverside coal yard. Major repairs and restoration were carried out in 1951 and 1960 when the domestic partitioning was removed and the last resident to live in any of the Bars was moved out at the time of the latter date.

The timber balustrade on the roof was renewed in 1968 and the heraldry, consisting of the Royal Arms, the York City Arms and the arms of Henry Vare on the outer side, wooden door and plaster projection were refurbished in 1978. In spite of its history of damage and continuous repairs Walmgate Bar is the only Bar to have retained its barbican, and there is still the portcullis and gates. In August 1980 the Bar was struck by lightning which caused serious damage that has subsequently been repaired.

Traitors' heads, including in 1469 Robert Hillyard (Hob of Holderness) and in 1663 one of the Farnley Wood conspirators, have been publicly displayed on this Bar.

The wall between Walmgate Bar and Fishergate Bar is mostly all

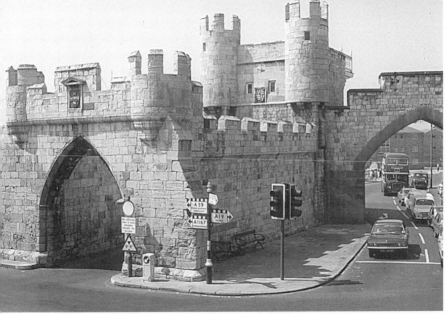

Figure 14. Walmgate Bar looking toward Walmgate.

of the nineteenth century rebuild although it is supported on what is likely to be the original wall plinth. The 'Wall Walk' has been rebuilt onto a solid wall with no arched supports in this length. Between tower 36 and Walmgate Bar the wall largely rests on a series of foundation arches the tops of some of which can be seen protruding above the top of the rampart. The plinth and arches are possibly original but the wall hereabouts to a height of some five metres is largely a reconstruction.

Red Tower, formerly known as 'Brimstone House' after a manufactory of gunpowder carried on within its walls, is the only part of the defences that was built in brick, having massive walls up to four feet thick (Figure 12). It was erected in 1490 and originally stood in the waters of the King's Fishpond and marked the re-start of the wall from that impassable swamp which reached from here to Layerthorpe Postern (Figure 13), the position

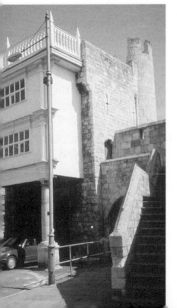

of which was near the existing Layerthorpe Bridge. The Red Tower suffered severe damage in the Siege of York in 1644. By the early eighteenth century it was in a ruinous condition but was then patched up for use as a stable about 1800. It was further restored to its present form in 1858 and was substantially renovated in 1958. The roof is of Roman tiles.

Tower thirty-five is of rectangular proportions and is six metres wide and projects just over one metre from the wall face.

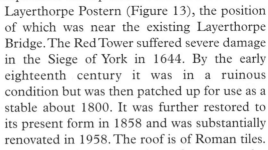

Figure 15. The rear of Walmgate Bar showing the sixteenth century extensions.

original. The length of wall in the vicinity of tower thirty-seven has probably been rebuilt at some time and the twenty metres leading up to Fishergate Bar containing no crenallations was probably rebuilt in 1487. Between the two Bars there are a number of buttresses irregularly spaced supporting the wall on its outer side. The outer rampart previously cut back to accommodate cattle pens in 1827 was reinstated in 1973 producing a considerably enhanced appearance.

Tower thirty-seven is the only interval tower between the two Bars. This is rectangular in plan being seven metres wide and projecting in part nearly two metres from the wall face. It has been filled in and possibly as a result of the rebuilding of the city wall at this point no longer appears to be bonded into it.

Fishergate Bar is now little more than an arched opening over the roadway with a small foot passage on either side. It was originally a substantial entrance containing a superstructure, portcullis, and possibly a barbican first mentioned in 1315. The towers over the gate were reduced in status during the reign of Queen Elizabeth I to that of a prison. On 15 May 1489 the Bar was burnt by rebels, and, when repaired, the arch was bricked up until 1827 when it was reopened to provide access to the newly built cattle market. Restoration to the Bar was carried out in 1961. The City Arms and the original plaque commemorating the 1487 rebuilding work of the adjacent wall were repainted in 1979, although both of these are now in a fairly advanced state of erosion.

In the Yorkshire Museum is a stone panel removed from the vicinity of the Bar that has the remains of a carved scene, probably of Sir Will Todd being knighted. This also carries the inscriptions *lx yerdis of length* and *Ao dni MCCClxxxvii Sir Will Tod mair* [mayor, knight and] *long tynme was schyrife* [sheriff] *dyd thys cost hyselfe*. The sixty yards of wall referred to in these inscriptions is possibly the section immediately adjacent to the east of the Bar.

The wall between Fishergate Bar and Fishergate Postern Tower follows an irregular alignment jutting out at tower thirty-nine to enclose a triangular area of land before doubling back to run down to the waters of the river Foss. This length of wall between the two was not built until 1345 and includes two interval towers.

Tower thirty-eight is rectangular in plan and measures just over two metres in width and projects one and a half metres

Figure 16. Fishergate Postern Tower.

from the wall face. Although it has not been filled in, there is now no access to the inside. The tower, at walkway level, is walled through by the Bar wall parapet, and this together with the construction of the tower suggests it was built onto the wall. The top of the tower has been stone flagged.

Tower thirty-nine is one of the more substantial of the interval towers. Although incorporated into the wall construction it projects considerably from it, and commands a dominant position in its corner situation. The tower contains a main room with a small alcove and a brick arched roof. Later adaptations to it include the insertion of a fireplace that in part remains, and two cruciform gun slits.

Fishergate Postern Tower at one time probably stood at the edge of the Foss (Figure 16). The present tower dates from about 1500 and replaced an earlier structure. When first constructed it was of two storeys with a flat roof and crenallated parapet. A roof was added in the sixteenth or seventeenth century to create a third storey. Restoration work to the tower was carried out in 1839 and appears to have involved considerable rebuilding work. In 1920 damage was caused to the fabric when it was struck by lightning. In 1960 further restoration was carried out on the tower.

Immediately adjacent to the tower is a small postern gateway. This is the only one of six original posterns constructed within the city wall to survive, although the superstructure supporting its portcullis no longer exists.

In medieval times the city defences were broken at Fishergate Postern Tower by the river Foss with York Castle towering over it on the far bank. The walls of the castle provided the necessary fortification and the city wall itself recommenced at Castlegate

Figure 17. Clifford's Tower from Tower Street.

Postern adjacent to the castle wall at Clifford's Tower (Figure 17) on the site of the present Tower Street. Although the postern gateway itself was removed in the year 1826 the length of wall running down to the river Ouse survives. This is a relatively low section of walling, deceptively so because of the rise in the adjoining ground level. It encloses Tower Place and terminates at Davy Tower at the South Esplanade. The surviving lower part of this tower is now incorporated into a modern private house.

The section of wall nearest to Tower Street for approximately thirty metres seems to be a rebuild, probably undertaken in the nineteenth century, but the remaining section running toward the river may well be original. The outer side of this whole length is flanked by a narrow public garden and for many years until recent times formed an impressive backcloth to a magnificent and colourful herbaceous flower display.

The original building of the walls was carried out by means of direct grants from the king. In 1226 the city was authorised to raise its own money for their construction and maintenance by way of *murage taxes,* which were tolls imposed on goods brought into York. Responsibility for the walls was shared between six wards into which the city was divided. Muremasters, usually four in number, were elected annually to see that the walls were kept in good repair.

The cost of maintaining the walls was later assumed by the City Council directly from its own funds and from the year 1585 until the present time all maintenance work has been undertaken by the 'Common Husband', or City Engineer and Surveyor as he subsequently became known.

Attitudes towards the preservation of the walls have altered with succeeding centuries. When the walls served as a means of defence they were presumably kept in a state of good repair. The advent of sophisticated artillery, however, spelt the end for the walls as an effective means of protecting the city from attack and in the latter half of the eighteenth century they gradually began to fall into decay. Fear of attack during the Jacobite uprising of 1745 led to the last real effort being made to prepare them as a defensive fortification. Thereafter the walls fell into total disuse and were largely abandoned and left open as pedestrian walkways. By the beginning of the nineteenth century the City Council was resolved to remove them altogether, partly on account of their crumbling and dangerous condition.

There sprang up, however, in the first two decades of the nineteenth century, a desire on the part of many citizens that the walls should be retained and preserved. This feeling led to the formation in 1827 of the York Footpath Association, a body of enthusiasts that was largely instrumental in launching a programme of restoration works to prevent any further deterioration. Extensive repairs and rebuilding subsequently went on for much of the remainder of the nineteenth century and culminated in the final section of the 'Wall Walk' from Bootham Bar to Monk Bar being opened to the public in 1889.

For the first half of the twentieth century repairs appear to have been carried out on a fairly limited scale with inexpert patching up carried out on a spasmodic basis. In 1922 the walls were scheduled as Ancient Monuments under the *Ancient Monument Act*, 1913 and by 1950 a far greater importance was being attached nationally to the need for a proper programme of preservation of ancient monuments that included, quite naturally, the city walls of York.

The year 1951 saw the formation in York of its own specialist team of masons to maintain the city's walls and monuments. This group of men has continued to enjoy a very high reputation across the country for the quality of its workmanship, and is almost certainly the leading team of stonemasons in England employed by any local authority. The results of their efforts can be enjoyed today by anyone who cares to walk along the city walls. This perambulation is perhaps one of the most enjoyable experiences in the whole of York's attractions (Figure 18). The length of the 'Wall Walk' is about two miles, and apart from the section of wall between Lendal Tower and Bootham Bar, the whole of the wall is now open as a free public promenade. Except in bad weather conditions they are open every day from eight o'clock in the morning until dusk.

Figure 18. A nineteenth century engraving showing the walls in a romantic light.

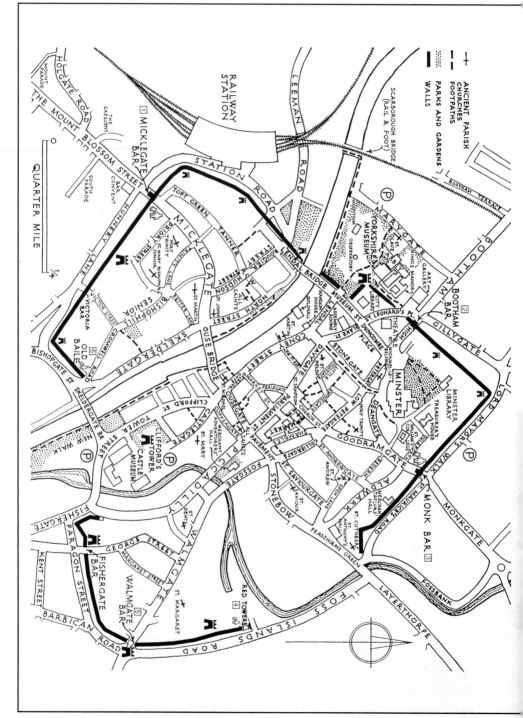

Figure 19. A street map of York centre showing the approximate position of the walls and indicating the main Bars.

12. FROM COUNTRY TO TOWN – GROWING UP IN YORK

by Eileen Rennison

WE MOVED FROM THE NORTH RIDING VILLAGE of Alne where I was born, to York, in March 1937, just a month before my tenth birthday (Figure 1). My Dad, whose part-time job was as a postman in a neighbouring village (Figure 2), was naturally pleased at the chance of a full-time position at the post office in York, but I remember being quite upset at the thought of a move and did not want to go. I was convinced that I would never see trees or green grass again, just endless buildings and paving stones.

Mum and my eldest sister, eleven years older than me, went off to York to find us somewhere to live. Very few working people owned their houses at that time and rented property was not too difficult to find. They came back full of enthusiasm for a house in Clifton that they had found, though a bit concerned about the rent of £3 a month, which was about twice as much as our house in the

Figure 1. The author (middle), sister and brother with dog outside their home at Alne.

Figure 2. The author's father wearing his postman's uniform in 1936 in the garden at Alne.

Figure 3. The new house in Clifton, 20 Avenue Terrace, as it is today.

village cost. But Mum said that she would manage it somehow and she was very good at making ends meet.

The day of the removal arrived and our belongings were packed into a large furniture van; a contrast to the horse and cart on which they had previously been transported when we had moved before from Back Lane to the Front Street. It was, despite my misgivings, impossible not to feel excited as well as a bit apprehensive.

When we arrived at York our new house was indeed in a terraced street with pavements and no grass verge, but we children could hardly wait to get inside the house and explore (Figure 3). It stood behind a privet hedge and wrought iron railings, which like all the others in the street were later taken for the war effort during the 1939-45 conflict. The house was a typical period town house. An inner door with brightly coloured stained glass panes led from the outer lobby into a hallway paved with patterned tiles. The staircase had a splendid mahogany banister down which I soon learned to slide! There were two large sitting-rooms, a living-kitchen with a black-leaded range like the one we'd been used to, a scullery with a sink and hot and cold taps - a novelty as we had only had a cold tap outside in the yard before - and a walk-in larder. The bathroom with its stained glass window meant we need no longer heat water to bath in a tin bath, and most wonderful of all, there were TWO flush toilets; one outside in the yard next to the coal-house and one upstairs with a mahogany seat and a fancy ceramic handle on the chain. No more going 'across the yard' with a candle after dark and my sister for company to keep the 'bogeymen' at bay!

The copper for boiling the clothes was in the scullery, so Mum no longer had to do the washing outside as she had before, with only a corrugated roof over the boiler and no walls for protection against the elements. It was still hard work though, scrubbing and 'possing', mangling, starching and ironing.

The house was originally erected for the builder of the row of houses for his own occupation and had a few extras that the other houses lacked. In the front room there were electric candles at each side of the mantelpiece, which seemed to a ten-year-old who had known for all but two of those years, only real candles and paraffin lamps, incredibly grand. In the back sitting-room a large sash window with two little opening doors beneath it, led into a conservatory. Upstairs, our house alone had a large wood panelled attic which, although it was only lit by a skylight in the roof, was reached by its own proper little staircase from what appeared like a cupboard on the landing.

The rooms in this house were more than in the old one, and we needed extra furniture. So Dad went to an auction and bought a large Victorian button-backed suite with a sofa, two armchairs and two upright chairs, all upholstered in red, for only £5. It fitted perfectly into one of the rooms and I thought it was very luxurious, but Mum was not too pleased and called it an 'ugly old-fashioned thing'.

We missed our huge garden in the country. The house had only a small yard, with a flower bed along one side in which to play, but we also played in the lane behind the houses. Cricket was a great favourite, with boys and girls playing together. Our wicket was chalked on a wall. The other children in the street often went to play in the 'Homestead' in Water End, the lovely park provided for Clifton by the Rowntree firm. It was not far away, but although we had been allowed to wander all over the village and walked alone to brownies in the next village, we were rarely allowed to go to the 'Homestead' without a lot of pleading. There was a grassed area for ball games and a playground with a chute and swings, also an aviary and some monkeys. After the enemy air-raid on York during the war they disappeared, though I can't remember whether they were actually bombed.

Dad had always grown all our potatoes, fruit and vegetables and missed the garden too. He took an allotment at the bottom of Burton Stone Lane and cycled down there in his spare time. He couldn't keep hens there, which we had always had, but at least we still got fresh produce and Dad still had the enjoyment of gardening. Later he rented the use of the garden behind a big house on Shipton Road which was nearer home and more convenient. He worked at the post office days and nights on alternate weeks, delivering and sorting. There were three deliveries of letters a day at that time and the postmen even worked on Christmas Day. Dad was never home to have his Christmas dinner with us.

He was not only a keen gardener, but could turn his hand to most practical jobs, as many people learnt to do, of necessity, in the 1930s. He made us toys from scrap materials, did woodwork, and could mend almost anything. He swept the chimney and always repaired our shoes. He even taught my sister and me to darn. When my brother fell and ran in with the broken ends of bone sticking out of his arm, Dad simply took hold and reset them, applied a splint and took him off to hospital where they said there was nothing for them to do! They couldn't improve on his handiwork. I don't know where he learnt all his skills. It was not from books. He was not a great reader.

One thing that had to be done as soon as we arrived in the city was to arrange our schooling. Mum took my sister, my brother and myself along to Shipton Street School. My sister had already taken the 'Scholarship Exam' as the 'Eleven Plus' was then not known, before we came to York and passed to go to Secondary School in September. We stood in the headmistress' study expecting to be told that we were all three to attend the school, but to our surprise she said she could take my sister and brother but not me. She didn't offer any explanation and I felt like a reject.

In the end I had to attend the North Riding County Council

Figure 4. Clifton-without-School as it is now with the colonnade closed in.

School (now Clifton Without Junior School) in Rawcliffe Lane on my own. The council housing estate in Water Lane was still under construction with the last few 'semis' (selling for around £400) in Fairway, being put up next to the school. The school itself was then very new and modern, built I think in 1935 or 1936. A long open colonnade (since closed in) ran alongside all the classrooms, which each had a fold-back wall of wood and glass opening on to it (Figure 4). This meant that on fine summer days we could be in the classroom and still have the benefit of fresh air. It was a big contrast to the old two-room, two-teacher village school I had been used to. There were forty-two children in my class alone!

I had to cope without my sister for support, but eventually I came to love it and was glad that I had to go there rather than the old-style school in Shipton Street. I did quite well there, though my family still tease me about one report I had that said - Mental - Weak. Sums of any kind were never my strongest point, but I did well enough to be awarded a prize of a paperback book, *Alice in Wonderland* for good progress at the end of the year. The only thing I did not like about school was that the boys seemed to be caned so often, not just for misbehaviour but for not knowing things, but that was the way it was in those days. The girls got rapped on the knuckles with a wooden ruler and I dreaded that it should ever happen to me, though luckily it never did.

At morning playtime we paid a halfpenny for a third of a pint of milk to drink. The small bottle had a waxed cardboard top with a centre hole that had to be pushed in to put the straw through. If you weren't careful and pushed too hard the milk would splash out everywhere. We saved and cleaned the bottle tops to make woollen 'pompoms' on. If one had a penny or a halfpenny there was a 'tuck shop' in a cupboard next to the headmistress' study, where we could buy sweets. In the playground the girls indulged in skipping and ball games against a wall, or hopscotch, while the boys seemed to play the sort of games that entailed a lot of rushing about and tussling.

One big event that took place while I was at school was the Coronation of King George VI. We spent quite a lot of time beforehand learning to sing *Land of Hope and Glory* and *I Vow to Thee my Country*, and on the occasion all the pupils were presented, not with the usual china mug, but with a commemorative beaker. Sadly I no longer have mine.

In the second year that I was there the school began to be overcrowded I suppose. Anyway, being a North Riding school, all those pupils who lived in York had to leave and find a place in a York

Figure 5. Form LIV at Mill Mount School on Sports Day, 19 June 1940. The author is fourth from the left.

school. I was allowed to stay on because I was due to take the 'Scholarship Exam'. This I duly did, and passed, and so was able to join my sister at Mill Mount School, which she had already attended for a year.

Dressed in our school uniform of navy blue gym-slip, cream blouse and red, yellow and navy striped tie and sash, topped with a navy gaberdine and felt hat, we walked from Clifton across the city to Mill Mount every day. We took a packed lunch for midday, although the school had its own cook and kitchen to provide hot dinners for about a shilling which were mostly taken by fee-payers of which there were quite a few at the school. Buses were frequent and fares only about a penny or 'tuppence', but with two of us at school bus fares and dinners would have been too expensive. Buses and bicycles were most people's means of transport. After my sister left school at sixteen to attend the School of Commerce, I made the journey on foot four times a day. People were used to walking in those times.

The legal school leaving age was fourteen, but if you passed the 'scholarship' you had to contract to stay until the age of sixteen. After taking my School Certificate at fifteen I stayed on in the sixth form for two years to take the Higher School Certificate (Figure 5).

After the Second World War began in September 1939 we were all issued with gas masks and had to carry them wherever we went, from classroom to classroom and even to the cloakroom. Our air-raid shelters were brick-built ones across the lane from the school building. I remember only once having to troop over there - it was a false alarm, or it may have just been a rehearsal. We amused ourselves singing and playing games. If the sirens had sounded during the night we were allowed to go to school later the next day.

When I was in the sixth form another girl and I sometimes fire-watched. Two members of staff and two girls were on duty every night. We never even had a false alarm when we were on, but I think we were paid a small sum of money which was the attraction. The staff slept in the Headmistress' study while we girls slept on camp beds in the secretary's room next door. Our only excitement occurred one night when mice ran over us in bed, but some girls used to entertain their boyfriends from Nunthorpe School surreptitiously in the kitchen, hiding them in the pantry when they heard the staff approach.

We had quite a lot of contact with the Nunthorpe boys. With their male staff going off to war some shared certain lessons with us. We also had a joint drama club and gave plays and held socials. We had ballroom dancing classes together and learned to dance to the records of Glen Miller and such tunes as *In the Mood*. At our first formal dance I slipped and fell and my full skirted dress went over my head to the cheers of all the boys; enough to put me off dancing forever! Dancing at the De Grey Rooms, to the music of Bert Keech and his band was popular, particularly with the airmen stationed at the many airfields around the city: Canadian, Free French, as well as our own boys from the Royal Air Force.

The Theatre Royal had a very strong repertory company with many actors who went on to become well known, among them Phyllis Calvert, Pauline Letts, John Alderton and Michael Rennie, who went to Hollywood. They presented a different play each week and I saw a good many of them from the 'Gods' for only fourpence. Companies such as Sadlers Wells, Ballet Rambert, and others toured the country during the war years to get away from the London 'Blitz', and I had my first experience of ballet and opera at this time. I fell in love with ballet when I saw Margot Fonteyn and Robert Helpmann in *Coppelia*.

In 1944 my sister and I took part as extras and chorus in a pageant

Figure 6. Festivals and pageants of various descriptions have long been a well-known aspect of York life.

staged at the theatre, in celebration of the centenary of the founding of the first Co-operative Society in Rochdale. We had great fun rehearsing, enjoying mixing with members of the 'rep' and learning what goes on behind the scenes at a theatre (Figure 6).

The most popular source of entertainment was the 'pictures' with long queues to get in especially on Saturday night. The performance was continuous and one had to pick up the story as best one could from the point at which you got in, then remain until it came around again. The commissionaire in his fancy uniform would stand outside calling 'Two seats in the one and three-pennies' or whatever became vacant.

There were ten cinemas in York; the Picture House, the Tower, St George's, the Electric, the Rialto, the Regent, the Grand, Odeon, the Clifton, and the Regal. The Picture House was in Coney Street where Woolworth's now stands. The Tower that was so small that it had only four rows in the balcony, was in New Street. St George's was built alongside Fairfax House and incorporated some of the rooms, having a stately ladies' room! The Electric in Fossgate - now a furniture store - was one where you entered under the screen. The Regent at Acomb and the Grand in Clarence Street were both also put to commercial use, though now only the Regent remains. The Odeon in Blossom Street with its art deco design is the only one of the original cinemas still showing films in the city.

The Clifton - now a bingo hall - was erected soon after we arrived in 1937. It had the first electric organ rising up in front of the screen and the first film it showed was *Sabu the Elephant Boy*. The Regal in Piccadilly was built later and also had an organ played by Austin Rayner, who went on to become a well-known organist on the radio. The cinema was no sooner opened than it was flooded. I recall sitting in a balcony seat looking down on the water shining in the stalls below.

Flooding from the river Ouse has always been a feature in various parts of York. Everyone remembers the awful winter of 1947 when the heavy snows led to severe flooding. The river came up Water End alongside Clifton Green and into the top of Water Lane. My niece who attended the little school next to Clifton Church was quite excited to have to be taken there by boat. Not so many people seem to remember the Ouse freezing over in 1940. My sister and I were egged on by two boys, after Sunday School, to walk across from Clifton Scope to the Leeman Road side. I was very scared because I couldn't swim but tried not to show it. The ice creaked loudly at every step but we made it across and back and were not the only people walking on the frozen waters. We attended Sunday School morning and afternoon well into our teenage years which may seem strange to today's youths, and often went for a walk with the boys up Shipton Road and back via the riverside on Clifton Ings, after the afternoon session.

In April 1942 the Germans made a bombing raid on York. Their target was apparently the railway and railway station but bombs and incendiaries fell over a wide area. Our street lay in line with the railway on the other side of the river and a bomb fell on the end of it. One house at each side of the road was destroyed and a large crater left in front of the gateway to the Fothergill Homes. Our windows were blown in, ceilings came down and roof tiles were blown off. The conservatory was completely destroyed. Tiny glass slivers pitted the furniture and the wall opposite the window in the front room that was nearest to the blast. Luckily at the time we were all in our indoor 'Morrison' shelter (like a large metal table under which we put a mattress to squat on) in the back room, all except Dad that is. He was working nights.

When the 'All Clear' sounded and we came out of the shelter, although we had been frightened, we couldn't help laughing. The soot had been blown down the chimney and into the shelter and we all had black faces. As we explored the devastated house we could see from the bathroom window that a house at the top of the street near the cinema was burning and also one of the boarding houses of St Peter's School, on the corner of the Avenue. When Dad came home from work in the early hours he was surprised to find my brother up there watching the firefighters. The next day people came around sightseeing and staring at the damage and into the house as if it was an exhibition, which upset me when we were doing our best to clear up the mess and restore some sort of order. Bands of tilers, plasterers, and builders were sent around the country repairing bomb damage and we were fairly soon restored to normal. There was even a mobile laundry in a large pantechnicon that came and parked in the street to wash any household linen, bedding or curtains dirtied in the raid.

In 1944 I left Mill Mount School and went to York School of Art. I had won a scholarship that paid my fees and a grant of £30 a year but materials had to be bought at the school shop. Sheets of cartridge paper cost one penny. We had a late start to the day at ten o'clock in the morning as long as the war lasted but the hours were long as we had to attend classes every evening from seven until nine o'clock and on Saturday mornings too. Students had to sign a time-sheet at the beginning of each session to show that they had attended on time. I'm afraid we sometimes cheated a little and signed for each other!

The Art School was housed to the right of the Art Gallery in Exhibition Square and when the school much later moved out to Dringhouses, the Gallery took over the rooms. What was our 'Life Room' is now the picture gallery to the right immediately up the stairs. Where the fountains are now situated, in front of Etty's statue, there was a large static water tank for use by the fire service during the war, and one night the students put a fishing rod into Etty's hand with a large cardboard fish dangling from it over the tank. It was quite a while before it was noticed and removed. As well as being York's famous painter, William Etty was also the founder of the York School of Art.

In architecture classes we often went sketching in the city streets. On other occasions York Races on the Knavesmire offered plenty of subjects to draw and another popular place was the Museum Gardens. It cost sixpence to gain entrance at that time, so Mr Cotterill, the Principal, would telephone through and get us admitted free. Once while sketching at York Station I was questioned by the police who thought I was a German spy!

It was not all work for us. Another student and I often organised parties in St William's College with everyone contributing to the cost (Figure 7). We had music, dancing and games. Our only drink was coffee and we would take the largest bowl we could find to Barton's cake shop in Bootham where they would fill it with trifle for half-a-crown. We had great fun, but it would no doubt seem very tame to today's students.

One year we held a very special St Valentine's Day dance at *Betty's*. Mr Bissell, vice-principal at the Art School did a large and wonderful

Figure 7. St William's College.

copy of Botticelli's *Venus*, with a splendid paper sculpture frame to decorate the ballroom. Dressed in a Grecian style robe and holding aloft a red heart I was pulled around on a little pedestal on wheels at one point in the evening feeling a bit foolish and very nervous.

Another social occasion in which I participated was the 'Georgian Ball' held in the Assembly Rooms on 15 June 1951 (Figure 8).[1] That was the year of the first York 'Festival' and the city that summer was alive with people and an air of excitement. There were concerts and entertainment of all kinds but the centrepiece of the 'Festival' were the Mystery Plays staged in the Museum Gardens against the back-cloth of the ruins of St Mary's Abbey. Mary Ure, then an unknown schoolgirl, who went on to become a well-known actress, took the part of the Virgin Mary. Only the part of Jesus was played by a professional actor, all the other members of the large cast were amateurs and local people. It was a wonderful and moving production.

I saw it only as a spectator but was determined to take an active part in the never to be forgotten 'Georgian Ball'. Tickets cost £6

Figure 8. The interior of the Assembly Rooms designed by Lord Burlington, 1730.

each, which was more than I earned in a week (I was teaching by then), but it was worth the scrimping and saving. My sister made my costume after studying my 'History of Fashion' books and scouring the shops for suitable but cheap material. I hired a hairpiece of ringlets and, with a group of friends, went off to the ball (Figure 9).

A crowd had gathered outside the Assembly Rooms to see the arrivals and we stood on the steps (Figure 10) and waved to them before disappearing inside to mix with the 'county' set! Dancing went on until the early hours when we were served a cup of soup before we left. I still have a faded rose, a

Figure 9. The author ready for the 'Georgian Ball' in 1951.

Figure 10. St Leonard's Place and the exterior of the Assembly Rooms (left). The new front was added in 1828 to the design of James Pritchett.

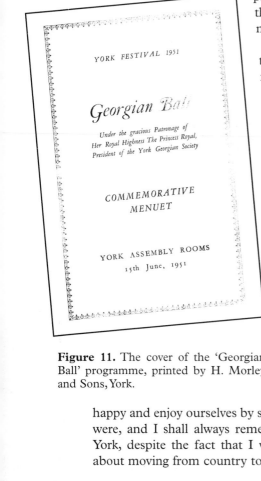

YORK FESTIVAL 1951

Georgian Ball

Under the gracious Patronage of
Her Royal Highness The Princess Royal,
President of the York Georgian Society

COMMEMORATIVE
MENUET

YORK ASSEMBLY ROOMS
15th June, 1951

Figure 11. The cover of the 'Georgian Ball' programme, printed by H. Morley and Sons, York.

programme (Figure 11) and the mask that was worn until midnight to remind me of a truly memorable evening.

The year 1951 was also, of course, the year of the Festival of Britain and my sister and I went up to London to visit it. This was the first time that I had been to the capital though my sister had been before. The Festival was a great experience with so many interesting things to see and do. I remember the Skylon towering upwards apparently without support, and Roland Emmett's Crazy Machine, and the Tree Walk that we went on. But there was much more. Even the fact that we had difficulty finding anywhere to spend the night could not detract from the visit.

There were certain restrictions in growing up at that period, mostly due to financial reasons and also the war, as well as the general ethos of the time. Many things have changed since then, however - but we always found ways to be happy and enjoy ourselves by simply making the best of things as they were, and I shall always remember with fondness my childhood in York, despite the fact that I was village born and had reservations about moving from country to town.

Notes and References

1 According to the programme it was held *Under the gracious Patronage of Her Royal Highness The Princes Royal, President of the York Georgian Society* and there was a 'Commemorative Menuet' *in honour of Lord Burlington, who designed these Assembly Rooms, and of those subscribers - about 200 in all - who, in 1730-5, provided funds for the building, the descendants or representatives of some of them will to-night dance a Commemorative Menuet.*

The names of those taking part are appended. Where the descendant cannot himself take part, he has nominated an anonymous deputy to represent him. The names of The Original Subscribers are as recorded by Francis Drake *in his* Eboracum (1736).

The arrangements for the Menuet *have been made by the Hon Mrs Forbes Adam and the Lady Deramore, on behalf of the Ladies Committee.*

The rehearsals have been carried out under the guidance of Miss E.M. Cooke-Yarborough.

The Menuet *will be danced at 11-30 o'clock. Later in the evening Miss Shirley Hall will sing a selection of songs from* The Beggar's Opera.

CONTRIBUTORS

1. ASPECTS OF YORK

Alma Brunton, was born in Middlesbrough. During her career she has been the manageress of a chemist in Middlesbrough, where her first husband had a senior position in the Dock Masters Office of Middlesbrough docks. His keen interest in fishing which he passed on to their only child Reginald (Reg), provided the inspiration for Alma's own interest in the sea. Moving to Whitby over twenty-five years ago, she managed Crockett's dry cleaners in the town for many years until her retirement. Later, after her husband died, she remarried and still lives in Whitby. Among her interests Alma lists writing, ballroom dancing, in which she has gained many medals and certificates, and cake decoration.

2. THE LOST MISERICORDS OF YORK MINSTER

Ben Chapman, woodcarver, artist, poet and social history writer was born in Kingston-upon-Hull in 1941. He has always had an interest in history, especially the medieval period and the eighteenth and nineteenth centuries. With his late wife Mave, he collaborated on a number of books as diverse as life in domestic service and pierrots. He has made several contributions to an international heraldic dictionary and his last book was on the subject of misericord carvings in Yorkshire churches. Ben is currently working on a large format picture book of misericords, a volume of animal poetry and a dictionary of bare-knuckle prize-fighting. He now resides in Withernsea and is a member of Withernsea Writers.

3. SPRINGTIME SAUNTERS
6. BRONZE PLAQUE GUIDE TO YORK
8. THE EARLY COACHING DAYS AND INNS OF YORK
11. THE WALLS AND BARS OF YORK

Alan Whitworth, trained at Bradford College of Art, but from 1977, after a number of years in the world of printing and graphic art, he predominately turned his attention to promoting the preservation of English parish churches, founding and running a charity to that end, writing and lecturing on the subject, mounting many exhibitions promoting the beauty of our homeland churches and organising the first national conference dealing with churches and tourism. And yet his interests are wider, and his regard for old buildings and history has led in one area to the founding of the Yorkshire Dovecote Society after a study of dovecotes and pigeon-lofts, about which he has written and lectured often, and in another, to compile a number of visual records about places with which he has been associated. He now writes and lectures about local history subjects and his books include *Exploring Churches* (in association 1986, 1993); *Yorkshire Windmills* (1991); *Village Tales - The Story of Scalby* (1993); *A History of Bradley* (1998) and *A Travellers Guide to the Esk Valley Railway* (1998) and numerous contributions to the Aspects series including *Aspects of Huddersfield, Barnsley, Rotherham, Doncaster* and others.

4. MAD, BAD AND DANGEROUS - JONATHAN MARTIN

Peter Howorth, a Lancastrian, settled in East Yorkshire after studying history at the University of Hull. He was awarded a M.Phil degree in history for research into aspects of local history and has lectured and written widely on the subject. After teaching in schools in Beverley, Driffield and Howden, he now lives in Driffield. Peter is the author of five books, including a *History of East Yorkshire Cricket* (1778-1914) and a biography of Luke White, the first working-class Member of Parliament to represent the East Riding.

5. A SHORT HISTORY OF THE BAR CONVENT

Sister Gregory Kirkus was born in York and educated at Newnham College, Cambridge. After taking a degree in history she joined the Institute of the Blessed Virgin Mary and held several teaching and administrative posts, including those of Headmistress at St Mary's, Shaftesbury, and Provincial Superior. She is now the librarian and archivist of the Bar Convent, York.

10. THOMAS COOKE : TELESCOPE MAKER OF YORK

Martin Lunn MBE was born in Surrey in 1957 and has had a lifelong interest in science. He moved to York in 1988, is married with three children, two boys and a girl. His career time is divided between being Curator of Astronomy at the Yorkshire Museum, in York, and taking travelling science exhibitions into schools all over Yorkshire. This is in addition to promoting science within the community through workshops and talks. His educational interests led the BBC to commission a book *Earth and Space* from Martin aimed at children. He has also had articles published on satellite technology and historical astronomy. In 1988 Martin Lunn was created an MBE for services to astronomy and education.

9. 'BOMBERS AWAY!' THE STORY OF RAF ELVINGTON

Ian Richardson was born in 1960 in Salisbury, Rhodesia. After emigrating from Africa to England in 1978, he worked mainly in the retail sector finally attaining the position of Section Manager with J. Sainsbury Plc. In 1995 he left his post to take up further education and graduated in 1999 with a HND in business from York University and then 2:1 (Hons) Degree in business management. He then joined the Yorkshire Air Museum as publicity officer following a course designed to help people seeking a career change. Ian is married.

12. FROM COUNTRY TO TOWN - GROWING UP IN YORK

Eileen Rennison was born in 1927 in a North Riding village and moved to York at the age of ten. Except briefly when first married she has lived all her life in Yorkshire. Educated at Mill Mount Grammar School and York School of Art, she qualified as a teacher of art at the College of Ripon and York St John and ended her teaching career as a lecturer there. She met her husband when they were art students and they have one son in the book-selling business and a married daughter, a German son-in-law and two granddaughters, living in Berlin. Eileen has written many articles on various subjects and three books on the curiosities of various parts of Yorkshire under the title *In Search of the Unusual* (Hutton Press).

GENERAL INDEX